HOW TO MAKE
A *GOOD* SONG
A *HIT* SONG

HOW TO MAKE
A *GOOD* SONG
A *HIT* SONG

Molly-Ann Leikin

BILLBOARD BOOKS
An imprint of Watson-Guptill Publications, New York

First published 1990 by Billboard Books, an imprint of Watson-Guptill Publications, a division of BPI Communications, Inc., 1515 Broadway, New York, NY 10036.

Library of Congress Cataloging-in-Publication Data

Leikin, Molly-Ann.
    How to make a good song a hit song / Molly-Ann Leikin.
        p.   cm.
    ISBN 0–8230–7561–3
    1. Popular music—Writing and publishing.   I. Title.
MT67.L33   1990
782.42164'13—dc20   90–35189
                                                                        CIP
                                                                        MN

Manufactured in the United States of America

First printing, 1990

1 2 3 4 5 6 7 8 9 / 95 94 93 92 91 90

For those of you who have been told "no" too many times,
this book is proof that it only takes one "yes."

Acknowledgments

I owe the following people lunch:

Barbara L. Adler
Jeff Barry
Lynn Benjamin
John Bettis
Stephen Bishop
Celestial Seasonings
   Peppermint Tea
Judith Claire
Christopher Cross
Hal David
Raymond G. "Hugs" David
Thomas Dolby
Ron Fierstein
Dr. Robin Futoran
Randy Goodrum
Lorie Gorman
Don Grierson
Louise Horvitz
James David Hinton
Bunny Hull
John Istel
Dale Kawashima
Anita Kruse
Dannie La Russo
Tad Lathrop

Lannie Levine
M&M's (with peanuts)
Alan Melina
Loretta Munoz
Alan O'Day
Dr. Bob Ohrling
Martin Page
Linda Perry
David Pomeranz
Diane Ponsher
Mr. Rightstein
Adryan Russ
Warren Seabury
Marti Sharron
Madeleine Smith
Paige Sober
John David Souther
Julie Speelman
Mark Speer
Billy Steinberg
Tom Sturgess
Suzanne Vega
Narada Michael Walden
and
Jimmy Webb.

Operators are standing by to take your calls.

Contents

PART THREE: DOING BUSINESS
IN THE MUSIC BUSINESS

APPENDIXES

Introduction

If you absolutely feel in your bones that you are a *good* songwriter, and if you're committed, focused, and determined to be a *hit* songwriter, this book's for you. Once you've journeyed through these pages you'll know exactly how to make your songwriting dreams come true.

I am a songwriting consultant in Santa Monica, California —my job is to turn developing songwriters into hit songwriters. I also work with hit songwriters who are in slumps and help put them back on the charts.

I work from experience—I have a platinum record, two gold records, an Emmy nomination, and four ASCAP Country Music Awards. I have written themes and songs for twenty-nine TV shows and movies, including "Eight Is Enough" and the Oscar-winning Short Feature *Violet.* I was a staffwriter for eight years at Almo Music (A&M), Interworld Music, and Chappell Music, and taught songwriting at UCLA. For three years, I wrote a regular column for the Los Angeles Showcase *Musepaper,* a monthly national songwriting magazine. I am the author of the beginning songwriting book *How to Write a Hit Song* (Hal Leonard Books). One of my readers nicknamed me the "Dr. Ruth of Rock 'n Roll."

More important than my own credits is the success enjoyed by so many of my clients who were "gettin' nowhere slow" *before* they came to me, and who are now making publishing deals as staffwriters and label deals as recording artists. One was nominated for a Grammy. Another won an Emmy. While I love to brag about my clients and *kvell* like a proud Jewish mother, the consultant-client relationship is confidential, and must remain as such. However, let me assure you that if my clients were not on the radio and in the record stores, my consulting business would've folded a long, long time ago.

In my career as a hit songwriter, I have experienced all the extremes of an artist's life—devastating defeat, ecstatic success, and everything in between. I've also witnessed my clients' endless frustrations and ensuing victories. So there's almost nothing that goes on in a developing songwriter's life that I don't know about, and for which I haven't offered a solution in this book.

As an undiscovered songwriter, you need more than a good song to get yourself noticed—you need a *great* song. This book was undertaken not only to improve and enhance songwriting in general, but to provide you with the means of creating your own *great* song. There is nothing anyone in the music business would rather hear than a hit.

Some songwriters feel their lack of success in the music business is the result of bad luck and lousy connections. That's part of it. Others feel if they sold the farm and moved to Los Angeles or Nashville or New York or London, their very presence would make record executives throw open the doors. However, the three *real* reasons for most songwriters' lack of success are:

1. The songs they write desperately need to be rewritten before being sent out into the marketplace;
2. They have no concept of how business should be conducted in the music business, and like most artists, suffer from being terrible business people;
3. They haven't learned to impersonalize rejection, negativity, and the intangible factors involved in bad timing.

This book offers valuable and viable industry solutions to all of the above problems.

To present as wide a perspective as possible on the intricasies of creating and marketing hit tunes, I interviewed thirty-seven of the best songwriters, singer/songwriters, music publishers, and A&R executives in the world. I've also included the most effective writing and marketing exercises I assign to my clients.

REACH BEYOND THE STARS

Developing writers beat their breasts blue with exasperation, unable to fathom why they're listening to other people's mediocre work on the airwaves when their own songs are better. The truly incensed will slip the "offending" songs onto my CD player and stand there defiantly, demanding a reasonable explanation as to how a well-known artist can record a song that's as exciting as grilled Velveeta on white bread and earn more money for it than the annual gross of the A&P, when a developing writer, whose song is just as good, can't make a kopek, or receive anything friendlier than a COD form letter from a post office box publisher in southern Tuscaloosa.

Let's put our cards on the table. This type of songwriter's exasperation is an ongoing problem, and it's important to discuss it.

Nobody became a *repeat* hit songwriter by being trite or by trying to get away with doing the least amount of work possible. Most artists establish themselves and their reputations by creating words and music that blow the tiles off the collective industry roof. Think of Bob Dylan's early songs. They were all originals. So were Elton John's. Bruce Springsteen's. Lionel Richie's. Tracy Chapman's. U2's. They didn't try to copy anybody and they weren't trying to make a fast buck and get out. They pulled all stops and went for it, with material nobody else was doing—no special-effect chartreuse smoke, snake makeup, or topless Eskimo backup singers in lavender glass G-strings. Each of these writer/artists has created a unique niche for him- or herself. What made room for them initially on the radio and on their labels' artist roster? The most important ingredient was the high level of writing and originality in their songs.

But like all artists, these writers hit peaks and valleys. Not everything Paul McCartney or Richard Marx or Stevie Wonder does is genius. They have some good creative days and bad creative days, just like the rest of us. The difference between them and an unknown act is that they're already established, so when DJs play their songs they know the audience is built in, and even if a particular record isn't brilliant, the next one may be.

It may seem unfair, but unknown writers can't be pretty good. They have to be better than *everybody* else.

From my point of view as a consultant, the solution to ending your obscurity and catching someone's ear is to make a deal with yourself—you're going to be a successful songwriter and if you have to be better than everybody else that is in line ahead of you in order to get your shot, fine. You will simply work harder, be more objective about your writing, and rewrite your songs until they're right. I believe that what got you into this business in the first place is the feeling that you have something original to say that nobody else has said yet, as well as a way to present your work that is just as special. So my suggestion is to stop complaining about the quality of the songs on the radio and improve the quality of your own material. In this way, a year from now when strangers all over the world turn on their radios and are raving about this new song or artist that blows them away, it'll be you and your music that they're so wild about.

Many developing songwriters come to me hot out of the studio with $20,000 worth of masters. Their relatives and the gang down at the day job just loved every tune on the tapes, and now these writers only need a list of managers in order to secure their three-record deal. But ninety-nine percent of the time, the songs I hear aren't finished yet. They're not ready for a manager or even a publisher to hear. They're good, but they're not great. They're not going to curl anybody's toes. They're not going to push another song (written by the artist himself) off an already-full album.

What most developing tunesmiths don't understand—or perhaps don't want to face—is that music publishers and A&R people are looking for songs and acts that dazzle.

I asked ten new clients to keep track of how they spent their time between our consulting sessions. They found they spent eighty-five percent of their days cutting tracks, not writing their songs. When a tape is rejected by a publisher, the production usually has little to do with it. It's the *song's* fault. Maybe it's a great idea, maybe it has a terrific first verse, maybe the chorus has a great hook, but where's the *rest* of the song? Maybe the title is so potent it could cure the common cold. Maybe the lyric has a few good lines in it. But that's not good enough. The song has to be one hundred percent there.

I suggest to anyone looking for a songwriting deal that instead of believing your break lies in finding heavy management, you backtrack a little. Make a deal with yourself to write five killer songs—not just five songs—but five "you-can't-say-no-to-*these*, -Clive" songs. Demo them with just one instrument, put them each away for a week, and then listen to see if they still fly. If they *almost* do, refine them until they're perfect. Then cut them and shop them.

Not withstanding all my disparaging comments about A&R people, even *they* cannot say "no" to a hit song. However, A&R people will wonder if the writers of that hit have more than one smash in them, because the commitment that a record label makes to a new act is substantial. If the A&R person hears two or three hits out of five songs, he/she has to get excited about that act. Your breakthrough will not be due to the muscle of a hot management firm that sends you on a tour of county fairs but to the integrity of the raw material.

Therefore, I recommend you do some career-course correcting and make the commitment to yourselves to yes, find the band, find the lead singer, find the engineer, find the gigs, but DON'T FORGET THE SONGS. Once you've got *them*, nothing can stop you.

That said, if you really want to be a hit songwriter—let's go to work.

PART
ONE

Rewriting

CHAPTER ONE

Rewriting

I want you to take comfort knowing that all songwriters hate rewriting. No matter how long they've been working at their craft, and in spite of how successful they have become, songwriters always feel violated by someone telling them that what they've created isn't perfect.

All writers feel the same way—novelists, poets, playwrights, and journalists. When my editor sent me his notes on the first draft of this book, even though accompanied by a glowing letter saying what a terrific job I'd done, I still had to hide in bed for four whole days before I could muster the courage to address myself to making the necessary changes.

For five years of weekday mornings I ate breakfast with a group of the world's most successful screenwriters at Marjan's Deli, in Brentwood, California. My breakfast companions were paid from $500,000 to over a million dollars per script, and collectively had more deals, Oscars, and Emmys than perhaps any other four writers who ever lived. You'd think with that kind of track record, they'd get used to rewriting. But it infuriated every one of them that they had to rework their screenplays, every time.

I wish I'd had a video camera to record the rage, rejection, desperation, and resentment each of these writers experienced every time he or she left a rewrite meeting. One poor guy who'd just won his second Academy Award, was so overwhelmed by the criticism of an early draft of a new script, he could barely eat his oatmeal and practically had to be spoon-fed by the waitress. Another writer, who was normally a perfect dresser (he could have moonlighted for megabucks as a model for Brooks Brothers), would show up after getting his rewrite "notes" wearing a mangy old sweater full of holes. So if you feel nasty, unwanted, rejected, and resentful when you have to do a rewrite, you're in good company.

The only writers who seem to get away without rewriting are singer/songwriters. They skip the prerequisite of having to please a publisher and an artist, usually because they are their own publishers, or at least copublishers, and they sing their own songs. All they have to do is please themselves. I'm not saying singer/songwriters' songs don't *need* to be rewritten. It's just that when producers and publishers hear a weak line, verse, or melody, most of them are reluctant to confront a self-contained act, especially a successful one, and say "that isn't good enough" or "take another run at it over the weekend, Elton."

I'd like to think the best of my singer/songwriting colleagues work as hard at writing songs and are as conscientious about their craft after ten years on the charts as they were when they were still scuffling and eager for recognition. Some of them are. My advice to all songwriters, no matter where they are in their careers, is to always write the best song they can, no matter how many drafts or weeks or demos or chiropractic adjustments it takes.

The need to rewrite a song comes from two motivational sources: external and internal. The former comes at the demand or request of someone else—a publisher, a collaborator, consultant, artist, or producer. The latter comes from within, when you hear yourself saying "this is close, but no cigar" as you turn the page and start another draft. Both are uncomfortable. Both are necessary.

YOU CAN'T FIX IT IN THE STUDIO

Before you say rewriting may be fine for other songwriters, but you don't have to rewrite your songs because you're going to fix them in the studio, let me assure you that you can't. All the whistles and tricks of 48 tracks won't help a song that doesn't work on its own.

"Oh," you plead, "I have a synthesizer and MIDI equipment and a drum machine and if you'd just give me a few days in the studio to cut a track before passing judgement, I'm sure I can fill up all the holes in my songs."

Sorry. A song is not just a track. It needs a melody on top of the rhythm and a lyric that accommodates both. Many of my clients and colleagues use their machines as crutches and their songs fall short. They spend their lives at their synthesizers, which they crank up loud, convinced they're mining gold at their consoles. But then, when these composers send out their songs for feedback, the material doesn't hold up, and they don't understand why.

The solution lies in using our imaginations. We can't expect a machine to do our work for us. A melody is a series of single notes. It has nothing to do with overdubbing and multi-tracking.

Music originates from feelings. Feelings come from your heart and creativity from your imagination—not from computers. Of course, once you hear a melody in your head, go to your synthesizer to embellish it. But before you do, make sure you have a song that works without all the tricks and electronics. Record it simply, with one voice singing the melody, accompanied by a single instrument—preferably a keyboard or guitar—playing the chords and rhythm. Put it away for a couple of days and then see if it flies. If it does, congratulations. Make your demo. But if your song doesn't work, it's rewrite time—sharpen your pencil and put on a pot of coffee.

Your songs have to work *before* you go into the studio. In order to decide whether your songs are ready to record or in need of rewriting, you have to ask yourself some hard questions:

- Can you remember the simple melody line and sing it back after hearing it only once?
- Do you start to sing the song in the shower without realizing you're singing it or hum it unwittingly in the middle of your day?

- Do your lyrics say something nobody else has ever said before?
- Is your song completely original or have you "borrowed" the melody or lyric or both from an already existing song?

If you can't answer affirmatively to all of the above, you have a rewrite ahead of you.

STARTING A REWRITE

It's important to begin a rewrite only after you've accepted the need for it. Approaching it halfheartedly will produce mediocre results. So if you're still fuming at someone turning your song down, someone who had the *gall* to suggest your chorus wasn't strong enough, don't start the rewrite yet. When you undertake it, you should have a clear head and be able to focus positive energy and attention on what the song could become, instead of how you're going to nuke its critics.

When you're ready to rewrite, do so in a comfortable, safe environment that's nurturing and nonthreatening. Most writers have an eccentric rewrite ritual. Wearing my favorite argyle socks, I curl up on my sofa with a heating pad, a pot of peppermint tea, and a fresh box of Nabisco cinnamon teddy grahams.

Some writers I know have to do their rewrites in bed, because they feel safest there. Others go to a favorite coffee shop. Still others get in their cars and drive for days, unaware of their location until they have to stop for gas, a fresh box of Nabisco cinnamon teddy grahams, or the night. Whatever works best for you, do it, no matter how bizarre it may seem. The end result— writing the best song you can—more than justifies the means. If it takes a shopping spree, or a bag of your favorite chocolate chip cookies to finish a hit, fine. With your royalties, you can hire a personal trainer to help you get back in shape. And your business manager will take care of the bills.

You might say that rewriting is all well and good for *other* writers, but you get your songs whole and perfect in the first draft. I understand the elation that comes from writing something in one shot, but the truth is most hits are the result of ten or twenty drafts.

But, you might argue, your girlfriend loves what you do. As do the assistant substitute part-time cashier at Music Plus, the mailman, and your mother. So why mess with success?

While it's nice to have the approval of this coterie of fans, they don't make the publishing and A&R decisions of the world. What you need to do once you have a draft of a song you feel is complete is *not* jump right into a massive, 48-track demo. Simply put your new song aside for awhile in order to distance yourself from it.

How long is awhile? Try three days. Hopefully, during that time, you'll become separate enough from what you've created to be able to view it objectively, see what else it might need, and discover where any weaknesses might lie.

I know writing is an obsessive process. I know it's hard disconnecting after the intensive rush you experience while creating. But writing is an art as well as a craft. Given time, you can replace a sloppy rhyme with a perfect one, and something original can come to you to take the place of a melodic cliché. So if you're just writing to try to make a quick buck, please do us both a favor and give your copy of this book to a songwriter who's really invested in writing great songs and having an important career.

Since you're obsessed with your song while writing it, you'll probably feel very let down, strung out, and unfocused when you put it away for a couple of days. I suggest you fight the urge to go back to it too soon. Make sure you do some physical exercise during this period. It will help you distract yourself from thinking about your song. If you spend your "distance time" going over and over what you wrote, you will have to tack a couple of extra days to the "waiting period" before you can go back to the next draft with a clear head.

Many songwriters are impatient to get their songs finished and aren't really concerned about the quality or longevity of what they created. There are virtually no points for speed—except for assignment writing for the movies or TV shows, when a theme is often needed a few hours before it's to be recorded. We're not after music by the pound here. Write one great tune every few months and you'll be light years ahead of where you would be if you just went for instant volume.

If you're still convinced that fast is fabulous, let's suppose you get one of your quickie songs cut. After the initial elation of getting a record (and who knows, maybe even a hit), just think how you'd feel if every time you heard it, you cringed at one spot in the bridge you only wished to God you'd fixed before it left your notebook. Unfortunately, by then, it'll be hopelessly too late to rewrite it.

If you think this could never happen, you're wrong. Lyricist John Bettis, who wrote dozens of hit songs for the Carpenters, confessed to me that in spite of the success of his lyrics, absolutely every time he hears a particular song of his on the radio, he still wishes he had one more draft.

Rewriting should not be viewed as necessary because you got the song "wrong." This isn't like taking your car to the repair shop, where you expect it be fixed perfectly in one day. Writing is a process. Each draft is part of that process. And with each draft, your song gets a little better and closer to what it eventually will be when it's finished.

There is a tendency among undiscovered songwriters to brag that they wrote a particular song in only three minutes or twenty minutes or even a couple of hours. Frankly, I don't need to be told—I can always tell when a song was put together in a hurry. You're no less a genius for taking the raw materials and reworking them, honing your craft, and creating something that's polished, professional, and perfect. Speed has nothing to do with excellence.

I used to believe adamantly that anybody who created anything in a hurry wasn't creating something of value. Then I watched a cable TV show about the superconscious, which is a mental state reached through very deep, intense concentration. It's where Carole King must've been when she wrote "You've Got a Friend" in one evening. But I don't want to mislead you. She had been writing hits for thirty years before this happened. Most beginning songwriters don't ever attain a superconscious state while they're writing. They are usually in too big a hurry.

When I met John David Souther ("You're Only Lonely," "New Kid in Town"), he told me his writing process is painfully slow. He remembers sitting with his guitar for six or eight months, waiting for something to emerge. Nothing did. Then one night his beautiful song "Silver Blue" came out whole. It is word for word and note for note the same version of the song I first heard Linda Ronstadt sing.

While it makes better press to say he wrote the song in one sitting, the truth is, the song was simmering for those eight months, probably in his superconscious. Until I experienced a superconscious flow myself, I thought the concept was a crock, since I always had to work very hard and dig for every line. But then, after not writing a single song for six years while I wrote screenplays, a gorgeous chorus melody came to me whole in my sleep. That made a believer out of me.

While a developing writer could rationalize finishing something in a hurry by claiming it came from his superconscious, the chances are it's a first draft at best, and ten or twenty more drafts are warranted before he can realistically say the song is finished.

All artists do many drafts before accepting a final version. Have you ever seen the sketches a painter makes before he finally picks up his brush? He must often work for weeks or months until he finds what he wants. This became particularly evident to me when I went to the Andrew Wyeth exhibit at the Los Angeles Country Art Museum and saw at least thirty studies for the now-famous Helga paintings. Those studies were Wyeth's rough drafts for the finished work we all know and admire. So, if a world-class painter can spend a year doing sketches before committing himself to a final portrait, surely a developing songwriter can do two or ten or twenty more drafts of a song.

I think of rewriting like redecorating. While you might wish you could impulsively run out in the middle of the night to a paint store and have all your walls redone in red by daybreak, the truth is, you restrain yourself. After you choose a color range, you probably bring home paint chips in different shades. Then you live with those paint chips for a few days until you make a decision. And even after you choose a color, which could be completely different from the one you originally wanted, you can still change your mind several times—even while applying the paint if the color seems too dark, too light, or clashes with your cat.

Many of the questions we ask ourselves during a redecorating process are applicable to rewriting: Does each new element fit with what you already have? Do you feel comfortable with the changes? Does the new look feel like it belongs with you? Does it stick out like a sore thumb? Would some other choice blend better, coordinate better? Harmonize better? And does it make the statement you really want to make?

While I hope you'll rewrite your songs with greater frequency than you'll repaint your walls, I feel the analogy works. If you think in these terms, it can really help ease you through the next rewrite.

As a consultant, I've seen that even the worst song, written by a rank amateur, often has something worth salvaging. When my clients ask for my help with a rewrite, I start by asking them what it is they want to say. Without the demand of having to make it fit the music or rhyme scheme, they'll tell me what they intended, and express themselves much more eloquently than they did in their song. My response is "then say that."

If you haven't said what you set out to say, but have a good line, save the line. Maybe it's the beginning of another song, or the springboard for one.

When rewriting, patience is important. While I am proud of being able to write in a hurry, I have taken as long as a year to finish a song. True, I did work on others in the meantime, but that one nagged at me until it was finished. I've also written a song on demand in a few hours, and even received an Emmy nomination for it. But frankly, I much prefer the luxury of time to go back and change a few conjunctions here and there.

Everybody has a different rewrite process. In each draft of everything I write, I always start over from the top, writing it neatly "in good," so the page is nice and orderly, friendly and inviting. Even when I'm working on the final draft, ninety-nine percent of the time I go back to it within a few hours or days and cross out a word and substitute another. Maybe all I need is an "if" instead of a "but," and as nitpicky as that may seem, the whole meaning of a lyric can change with a new preposition or conjunction.

Just because you're in a hurry to finish something doesn't mean your muse is on the same timetable. Think of your muse as your partner, and make peace with her agenda. Anytime I'm stuck, I try to remind myself that if I got this far in a song, surely the rest is out there somewhere on its way into my head. I assume inspiration is coming, and try not to force its early arrival.

While waiting, I try to make my mind fertile and orderly. Just as I tidy up my house before a very welcome guest arrives, before I write I'll often vacuum, clean up the kitchen, dust, put some fresh flowers in a pretty vase on the table. I don't *need* to do this—I have a housekeeper. But these activities create a very positive, welcome environment for my guest—my muse. I want my imagination and my creativity to feel as ready and as receptive to new ideas as my house does to company.

HOW TO PROCEED

When you're ready to start a rewrite, and if you've been lucky enough to find a professional critic (a consultant, publisher, producer, or even a singer) who has told you specifically what he or she didn't like about your song and wants changed, write that at the top of your rewrite page. "She wants the second verse to be more emotional," for example. Then each time you get an idea, scribble it down and see if it is more emotional. If it is, good; if it isn't, don't cross it out. Keep writing. The more ideas you have, the more you will get. Don't refuse to write something down because the critic in your head has hated everything you've done since you weren't snapped up by the firm of Instantly, Famous & Rich, a Professional Corporation.

It's important for you to make peace with the rewriting process. As long as you're a writer, you'll never *not* have to redo what you've done, so the sooner you accept that, the better off you'll be. But don't expect to reach nirvana by sundown. Learning to rewrite is like learning to do anything—you acquire the skill slowly.

Please note that the following rewrite warm-up exercises are just exercises. The point in doing them is not to write hits, but to ease you into the rewrite process.

EXERCISE ONE

I find that writing something that doesn't count makes a terrific warm-up exercise. Something that's silly and whimsical is even better. So here's a suggestion that's both: rewrite "Mary Had a Little Lamb." In case you've forgotten, the original version goes like this:

> Mary had a little lamb
> Little lamb, little lamb
> Mary had a little lamb
> Whose fleece was white as snow.
>
> He followed her to school one day
> School one day, school one day
> He followed her to school one day
> Which was against the rules.
>
> It made the children laugh and play
> Laugh and play, laugh and play
> It made the children laugh and play
> To see a lamb at school.

After you get over the shock of having to tamper with a childhood memory, consider the possibilities: Mary had a little pig. Or if you're kosher, Mary had a little goat. Or Mary had fourteen Big Macs. It all sounds terribly awkward at first, but that's only because you're used to it the old way.

In addition to being fun while helping you gentle yourself into a rewrite, the purpose of this exercise is to show you that no matter how sacred, no matter how fixed in your mind a song is, it can always be changed. The original line in Oscar Hammerstein II's lyric "Oh What a Beautiful Morning" was "the corn is as high as a cow pony's eye." Then he realized that a cow pony wasn't tall enough. So he substituted "elephant," which was a taller animal with three syllables. "Cow pony" sounds awkward now, but we would've gotten used to it if Hammerstein didn't know he had a height problem.

Your task here is to write "Mary Had a Little Lamb" as a verse/chorus song. Right now it has an AAA structure (each section has the same form). If it were verse/chorus it might go like this:

VERSE
Mary had a little lamb,
Little lamb, little lamb
Mary had a little lamb
Whose fleece was white as snow

CHORUS
And it went baa baa baa
baa baa baa boo
yes it went baa baa baa baa
can you?

VERSE
It followed her to school one day
School one day, school one day
It followed her to school one day
Which was against the rules.

CHORUS
'Cause it went baa baa baa . . .

The next time you resist rewriting, take something as silly as this and play with the rewrite.

EXERCISE TWO

Now that you're rolling, you can do anything. I suggest you try rewriting "Ring Around the Rosie." The original nursery rhyme goes like this:

Ring around the rosie
A pocket full of posies
Husha husha
We all fall down.

Perhaps the first thing to do would be to make the last line rhyme with "rosie." How about, "I fell inside the bosie"? But, you might say, that doesn't make sense. True. But does any of the rest of it?

Go ahead. Take some chances. Write a completely new version of this nursery rhyme. You might want to give it a new title. How about "Ring Around the Collar"?

EXERCISE THREE

Write a parody of a hit song. I love to do that. Goldman, an old friend of mine, was nominated for an Oscar, and everybody was sending him huge baskets of fancy food. This was at the time when "We Are the World" was a big hit. Smart ass that I am, I realized that while the rest of the world was sending food to Ethiopia, people in the movie business were sending it to Beverly Hills. So instead of the original "We are the world, we are the children," I started singing "We are the world, we are the Goldmans." My friend got a big kick out of it, I got to exercise my rewrite muscles, and everybody was happy.

Take a song you hear on the radio and rewrite the lyrics. Change the subject matter completely. Start with the title. Make it fun. Visual. Most of all, don't write it "to count." Write it just to enjoy the process of writing.

Producing parodies has paid off for "Weird Al" Yankovic. I'm not suggesting you duplicate what he's done—adapting Bruce Springsteen's "Born in the USA" into "Born in East L.A." or Michael Jackson's "Beat It" into your own top 40 hit, "Eat It." But if you can write something silly, you're still writing. And once you're writing and feeling creative, the positive energy from that experience should spill over into something you really do need to rewrite.

I've often wanted to rewrite our national anthem. How audacious, you might say. Who does she think she is? Well, "Whose broad stripes and bright stars" doesn't sing. We all stumble over those words every time we sing them. The lyric is clumsy. Period. Francis Scott Key could have written "and the stripes and the stars" which isn't as visual or poetic but it sure does flow off our tongues better. Please—I don't want any cards and letters from the Daughters of the American Revolution telling me I'm a commie rat fink traitor. Ask any established songwriter or singer about the problems in the lyrics to "The Star Spangled Banner" and I guarantee he/she will agree with me. Remember, no song is beyond rewriting.

For a whole year, Paul Williams had to do draft after draft of his lyric for "Evergreen." He said it was only finally finished when Barbra Streisand, a known perfectionist, finally ran out of time and had to record whatever umteenth draft Paul had rewritten. The song won an Oscar, with Streisand sharing credit as a collaborator, but I believe any of his earlier drafts would have garnered as much acclaim as the last. But Paul is a professional lyricist—he knows that if a collaborator insists on a rewrite, you keep working. He could've quit, but consider this: he went home with an Academy Award, not an orphan lyric without a tune. Had Williams walked out, Streisand could have easily gotten somebody else who was more flexible about rewriting endlessly.

Spending a year reworking one tune may seem like an extreme case, but look what happened to Paul Williams. If you sense a song is bound for greatness, don't walk away from it, no matter how ludicrous the need to rewrite may seem.

CHAPTER TWO

Editing Your Songs

In most of the *first* songs that my clients send me, the lyrics are too bulky, and consequently, the melodies are too cluttered. When that happens, it's almost impossible for the melody to be memorable. And since the tune is the part that has to grab us first, the lyric has to defer to the needs of the melody. Often in the arts we say "less is more." This means it's important to weed out what's unnecessary and keep only what you absolutely need.

Most great writers have to make painful editorial decisions all the time, so if editing is hard for you, you're in good company. It's probably easier to chop off your finger than it is to eliminate a line or phrase you love. However, if such a phrase needs to be cut, whether it's lyrical or melodic—edit it out, and put it in the separate book of ideas you're saving to use in other songs. In this way, whether or not you ever use the phrases you cut, you won't feel that you're losing them completely.

If editing is a problem for you, imagine you're buying each syllable or note with a hundred- or thousand-dollar bill, depending on your budget. Sheer economics will dictate whether a word or a note stays or goes.

If you write lyrics only or melodies only, do all of the exercises anyway. I didn't say your results had to be hits—I just want you to have the practice. You never know when you'll be in a collaborative situation where something is too bulky and needs

trimming. Once you've gotten some practice here, you can transfer that experience to a real situation later.

EXERCISE ONE

A lyric you've had in your portfolio for years is harder to rewrite
than one you're just working on for practice, so rather than have
you rewrite something of your own, here's a rewrite/edit exercise that won't upset your ego or violate the integrity of any your
songs, because I'm using lyrics I just made up. You'll find the
syllable count at the end of each line.

> Oh, if only I could find a way to be there with you
>   tonight (16)
> Then I would be the happiest person on the planet earth (15)
> Happier than a guy who wins the California lottery (16)
> And doesn't have to wait twenty years for it, but gets it all
>   immediately (20)

I made this verse clumsy and cluttered and unsingable on
purpose. If a client brought this to me and asked me to help him
rewrite it, I'd first suggest he cut the syllable count by at least
fifty percent, maybe even more.

So as an exercise, do that now. Keep the message of the lyric
basically the same. You might want to try it five or six or thirty
times before you're happy with it. Do the best you can in ten
minutes. Remember, we're just doing this for practice, not prizes.
Here's what I came up with:

> If you were here with me (6)
> Winning the lottery (6)
> Wouldn't feel half as good (6)

You'll notice I left out the part about getting all the money
at once and not waiting twenty years. I omitted it on purpose,
since I felt it was unnecessary—you get the idea without it. I also
omitted "California," since, although the proper noun suggests a

picture, and I usually love images, the word has five syllables. Five syllables that clutter up a line are five too many. Besides, a lottery is a lottery. Many states have them—winning any state lottery would be a windfall. It isn't like California's is a gambler's only chance.

Please note that while I didn't get to say everything in the rewritten lyric that I did in the first, I said enough to get the point across. And I said what I had to say in eighteen syllables, not fifty-six.

Also notice that in my rewrite, I ended up with a three-line verse, not four. Some songwriters insist their verses be meticulously symmetrical, always having four lines and eight bars. A beginning composition teacher might smack my hands with a ruler for suggesting this, but I feel that by making the number and length of the lines in each verse irregular, the song has many more surprises, and is therefore a better song.

You might argue that if this were your song and it already had a melody, or worse, if you'd already cut an expensive, time-consuming track, you'd have to scrap the whole tune. Frankly, dear, that's too bad. I know it sounds cold and bitchy, but you should know right now, that at best, rewriting is inconvenient. I guarantee if there were a melody to the cluttered, original fifty-six syllable verse, the tune would be totally forgettable. But if you write a melody to the concise, succinct, little eighteen syllable verse that I rewrote, the tune would have a better chance of being terrific.

EXERCISE TWO

Write a melody either to my rewrite or to your own. Don't feel you have to shoot for Chopin—just create something that goes with the rhythm of the lyric. Try to make it sound as romantic and sincere as the words. Tape your melody. Twenty-four tracks aren't necessary. One will do fine. Then listen back, asking yourself some tough questions.

Can you sing your tune after hearing it once? You should be able to.

Have you "borrowed" the tune from someone else's melody, or is it brand new? It should be original. Save yourself the aggravation and frustration of a copyright infringement suit —if your melody sounds like another tune, change it immediately. Even if the composer you ripped off is long dead, some heir to the estate, wearing a blue plaid polyester leisure suit like those often seen at ASCAP meetings, will easily hear the similarity, sue you, and win.

Does your melody surprise you? It's supposed to. If it doesn't, rewrite it so it's not quite so predictable. And I don't mean changing a few chords or fiddling with the arrangement. To test your work, play the melody one note at a time on the piano with your right hand. That's the toughest test any song will have to pass. If your tune works with one finger on a keyboard, or when whistled, hummed, or "la-la'd" a cappella, then you've really got something worth keeping.

I know that many of you who "write" on guitars only play chords and don't know how to pick out a song's individual notes. I believe that's the reason so few great melodies are written on guitars. Most guitar composers "write" chord patterns and rhythm patterns, *not* melodies, and then settle for a tune that they squeeze out between the chords. I ask my guitar composer clients to try switching to a keyboard for this rewrite exercise— even if it's just an inexpensive, one-octave portable. If that's unthinkable for you because of ego, expense, or because you miss the intimacy you feel holding your guitar in your arms as you create, just "hear" your melody in your head and hum or whistle it into a tape recorder. Then rewind and listen to it and ask yourself my three tune-testing questions—if you pass, proceed to the next exercise.

EXERCISE THREE

Let's try another editing job. This time your goal is to cut the syllable count of a verse at least by half. Since I'm asking you to do something you don't enjoy, I'll choose a subject I hate—

football—so we'll all be miserable together. Don't accuse me of being self-indulgent, even if it is *my* book.

> If Notre Dame University's quarterback fumbled the football on the twenty yard line (23)
> The University of Southern California Trojans could win the Rose Bowl just fine (22)
> And maybe, since the odds were favoring all underdogs today (16)
> You'd finally smile back when I looked your way. (11)

Here's my rewrite:

> If Notre Dame blows it and the Trojan's win (11)
> It's a red and gold Rose Bowl we'll see (9)
> And if it's finally the underdog's day (11)
> Maybe you'll love me. (5)

I purposely made the first and third lines the same length with the same stressed syllables, because that way, a rhythm pattern is suggested in those lines. But I also purposely made the second and fourth lines different lengths so you wouldn't hear what you were expecting. Try not to lose that element of surprise when you edit my football song. Make sure it's thirty-six syllables or less.

EXERCISE FOUR

Make up a new verse—about any subject. Make it three to five lines long. Do a new verse about a different subject every day for a week, being careful to keep the syllable count low. By the end of the week you should be comfortable with using fewer words to say what you really mean. Plus, you'll have at least seven new song ideas.

EXERCISE FIVE

Write melodies to each of the new verses you created. You should notice how easy it is to write a catchy melody when the lyrics are simple and direct. And save your work. You never can tell if a fragment you write will grow into a hit verse or chorus down the road.

CHAPTER THREE

Say Something New

Even though you may hear many hits on the radio that are burdened with clichés, it's important for you to write songs with lyrics that are unique. As talented as you may be, nobody knows you yet, so you have to present yourself in the best possible light. You have to write better songs than those on the radio.

If you find that intimidating, please, don't let it be. Just as there's nobody in the world exactly like you, there's nobody in the world who writes like you. Each writer should develop his or her own "signature," or particular style of writing, so when someone hears one of that writer's songs, the listener will say "I bet so-and-so wrote that." If you're just copying what fifty people before you have done, that won't ever happen.

But I have lots of suggestions to help you develop your lyrics so they really do say something new. Consider this: each time we fall in love, we feel things we claim to have never felt before. Even if it's our tenth husband or fourteenth Significant Other. So don't our new relationships deserve to be chronicled in lyrics that have never been used before?

There are lots of ways of making your words original, as the next chapters will illustrate. But one of the biggest problems with most of the lyrics that cross my desk is that their individuality has been crippled by clichés.

"You're my everything" is one of the most frequent offenders. No man in my life ever had an "everything." I think they all had them removed at birth. "It's clear to see" is another phrase that's been overused, along with it's first cousin, "I was too blind to see." (You're either blind or you're not—there's no in between.) Other common songwriting clichés are "I need you like flowers need the rain" and "you're my sunshine." A cliché immediately warns me that a writer is making choices too easily, simply repeating what everyone else has already said. Think of it this way: why should you get the money when I buy the recordings of your songs? Shouldn't the royalties go to the first guy who wrote the phrase you "borrowed"?

I've always fought against clichés. In 1989 I was so fed up with the pesky critters I went to a patent attorney to trademark a new product I invented called Cliché Control. It comes in a spray bottle, and you apply the formula to your lyrics. If the clichés don't disappear after application, the instructions read: "Spray again. If clichés persist, rewrite. Spray again. If clichés aren't gone within seven days, call my office."

Eliminating clichés is my biggest passion (along with campaigning to rid my neighborhood of the Doberman next door). So it was appropriate that last Christmas, a writer from Santa Barbara sent me a calendar in which each day of the year was represented by a different cliché, plus the source and date of its original use. I feel it's important for you to read through the list carefully, to see who your "collaborators" have been all these years. Turn to the appendix on p. 153 to get an idea of how persistent and pervasive these pests are. Keep the list handy and check every one of your songs against it.

To give you a taste of what you'll find in any list of clichés, I've included a few of the more popular ones below. I bet you'll recognize most of them from the lyrics of some of your favorite top 40 tunes:

"Actions speak louder than words"—Gersham Bulkeley, *Will and Doom* (1692).
"Big as all outdoors"—John Neal, *Brother Jonathan* (1825).
"Clear as a bell"—Leminus, *Touchstone of Complexions* (1565).
"Dead and gone"—William Shakespeare, *Hamlet* (1603).

"Every cloud has a silver lining"—John Milton, *Comus* (1634).
"Find it in their hearts"—Thomas More, *Utopia* (1551).
"Grind to a halt"—Harriet Martineau, *Society in America* (1837).
"Heart of gold"—William Shakespeare, *King Henry V* (1600).
"Off the deep end"—Christopher Morley, *Kitty Foyle* (1939).
"Place in the sun"—Basil Kennet, *Pascal's Thoughts* (1727).
"Play with fire"—George Whetstone, *Heptameron* (1582).
"Ships that pass in the night"—Henry W. Longfellow, *Tales of a Wayside* (1863).

EXERCISE

Write a song *without* any clichés in it, and *without* the twenty-five most overused words in pop songs, which include "love," "heart," "touch," "baby," "need," "want," "hurt," "morning light," "together," "forever," "miss," "kiss," "hold," "arms," "smile," "dream," "dance," "eyes," "understand," "hand," "alone," and "lonely."

I suggest you make your song silly and playful, so it doesn't "count" or feel like such a tremendous demand on you. Perhaps you'll want to write about a cat named Spot who barked, or Kareem Abdul Jabbar's past life experience as a midget, or the volatility of hog futures. As long as you write a song, any song, no matter how ridiculous it may sound, by following the rules of this exercise, you'll see you *can* do it. And once you've gotten practice with a song that doesn't count, you can start applying your new cliché-free ideas to the "real" songs you write from here on.

CHAPTER FOUR

How to Write Great Opening Lines

Now that you've eliminated clichés from your lyrics, it's time to turn your attention to embellishing and enriching these lyrics. Just as a day that starts out well usually continues well, a song with a great opening line is destined for a better future than one that starts poorly.

Jeff Barry ("Da Doo Ron Ron," "I Honestly Love You"), told me he feels most developing songwriters waste the first verse warming up and don't really get to the meat of what they want to say until the second verse. I agree with him. The only warm-up time you get in a song is the four instrumental bars you're allowed as your introduction. When the verse begins, you should start your story immediately. And the line with which you start should be dazzling.

Let me give you an illustration. Imagine yourself at a fancy sunset party on a San Francisco rooftop. You're all dressed up and feeling ready for some romance. Before you know it, a dark-haired, green-eyed, well-dressed partygoer takes two champagne flutes from the waiter's tray and hands one to you, and says, "You live around here?"

What a letdown. You can't ever remember being so disappointed by a cliché. "I'm a Gemini," your budding conversationalist adds. "And I drive a 320i convertible. What about you?"

I don't know about your reaction, but I'd be completely turned off. That's why Leikin's First Law of Successful Songwriting is: Banality Bombs.

Now, let's suppose the party scene played out differently. It's the same rooftop, the same sunset, and the same person with the delicious eyes who smiles at you and this time whispers, "Last night I dreamt I was flying over Bordeaux in a hot air balloon and you were there in the gondola with me."

That's more like it! See the difference? It's much easier to get hooked by originality.

One of the rules of screenwriting is that you have to tell your audience what your story is about in the first two minutes. You have eight more to set up the conflict. Most films are approximately 100 minutes long. That means we need to know the subject and conflict of the story within the first tenth of the movie.

Let's apply this ratio to songs. Since an average song is usually two and a half minutes long, that leaves the songwriter the first fifteen seconds, or first two lines, to introduce both the subject and set up the story.

There are some classic examples in the literature of music that illustrate this well. "Manic Monday," written by Prince and sung by the Bangles, begins "Six o'clock already I was right in the middle of a dream/I was kissing Valentino by a crystal blue Italian stream." We all identify with the feeling of not wanting to get up to go to work—especially when we have a good dream going. This fantasy wasn't with just any surfer, but Rudolph Valentino, the world's greatest lover. And it wasn't happening in the back of a Chevy Blazer, either, but near a clear, blue stream somewhere in Italy. Who'd want to leave that and go rotate tires for Mark C. Bloome, the California tire king?

In "Ode to Billy Joe," the first two lines are "It was the third of June, another sleepy, dusty, delta day/I was out choppin' cotton and my brother was bailin' hay." Right off the bat, we're given the season—summer—when things are sleepy and dusty. We have a location—somewhere on a backroad delta, which, we assume, is in the southern USA. We see people in cotton fields and other workers on hay wagons. We're placed in a low socio-economic setting too, since picking cotton isn't a great paying job. And all that in just two lines.

Bobbie Gentry, who wrote this song, hooks us early with fresh vocabulary and takes us right to the heart of her song, setting it up so we're *in* it from the first phrase. We see what she sees and feels what she feels. And it's new to us. We don't have to wait for the third verse for impact or originality. She gets us in the first *two* lines.

You may be put off with my reaching back so far in musical history for this example, but I believe if a song sets a standard for excellence, it remains a great model, even though musical styles change. Bruce Hornsby begins his song, "Mandolin Rain," with "The storm came and went like the time that we spent/ hiding out from the rain under the carnival tent." Great simile. Good writing.

"Ruby Red Dress," written by Linda Laurie, and one of Helen Reddy's biggest hits, has two great opening lines. "She's forty-one and her daddy still calls her baby/Everyone 'round Brownsville says she's crazy." Bingo. We have an aging weirdo. In small-town Texas. This female character is an original. We keep on listening because we want to know more about her. Every line of the lyric adds to our fascination about the woman.

Remember "Angie Baby"? "She lives her life in the songs she hears on the rock 'n roll radio/And when a young girl doesn't have any friends that's a pretty nice place to go." Alan O'Day introduced us immediately to the heroine of his song, who lived vicariously through the music she loved, and into which she eventually disappeared. What makes it really work is that Alan got into the song quickly with an idea that was unusual. There had been millions of songs prior to this one that sang about the symbiosis of singer and song, but it was the element of magic that was introduced in this one that kept it from being a cliché.

"I was born in the wagon of a travelin' show/My momma had to dance for the money they'd throw" are the first two lines of John Durrill's "Gypsies, Tramps and Thieves." These lyrics really take us off on an adventure. We can immediately see images associated with a traveling gypsy show—a barker with a top hat, a rickety, painted, horse-drawn wagon, and a dark-skinned gypsy woman in a brightly colored, tattered skirt, dancing with a tambourine, while people look on, tossing their money at her. John didn't waste a syllable. His words are so bright, unusual, and dazzling, we couldn't possibly *not* listen to them.

A song that establishes great emotional intensity from the first note is "Sometimes When We Touch," written by Dan Hill and Barry Mann. "You ask me if I love you and I choke on my reply/I'd rather hurt you honestly than mislead you with a lie." You know immediately that this song is not just another "miss-you-baby while-I'm-here-alone-prone-stoned-by-the-phone" song. It's special because it starts off being dangerously honest, using vocabulary that we don't often say to one another, and which hadn't yet been sung.

Other favorite opening lines that stay on my top ten include "It's nine o'clock on a Saturday, the regular crowd shuffles in/ There's an old man sitting next to me making love to his tonic and gin." That is how Billy Joel introduced us to "Piano Man," his first big hit. Notice that he didn't waste a syllable. He brought us right there, immediately setting the time and place, and filling the stools around his piano bar.

One of my favorite country songs begins, "Woke up this morning, put the TV news show on/Bryant Gumbel was talkin' 'bout the fighting in Lebanon." This song starts by describing the way a lot of us begin each weekday—by tuning in to the "Today Show" and seeing what's happening in the world. Millions of people *see* Bryant Gumbel every morning, but nobody had ever *sung* about him before this tune. When this record was released, most Americans had heard about Lebanon on newscasts and read about it in newspapers for years, but nobody had ever used this Middle Eastern battleground in a lyric until Rory Burke, Charlie Black, and Tommy Rocco did in the opening lines to their song "A Little Good News."

The song "Don't Shed a Tear," sung by Paul Carrack and written by Eddie Schwartz and Robert Friedman, starts off: "Cab fare to no where is what you are/A white line to an exit sign is what you are." No mistaking that the guy thinks *this* relationship is over.

I'm especially fond of Melissa Etheridge's song "No Souvenirs," which begins "Hello, hello—this is Romeo/Callin' from a jackpot telephone." The phrase "jackpot telephone" is a killer. Nobody's ever used it before and it sure makes you want to hear the rest of the song.

Strong first lines have another function, too, because if you start off a lyric well, you have to try to make each line as strong as the opening few. Then the whole song will be terrific—not just a random accidental line here and there. Use the lyrics that dazzle you as your models—not those flabby, clichéd tunes penned by singer/writers who happen to be hot and who could release an unmarked CD of their babies burping and it would still ship platinum.

Write opening lines that are fresh and surprising and that will catch the listener's ear. The audience you're trying to reach at this stage of your writing life is made up of publishers, producers, and A&R people. They've been bored by all the clichés, so if you come out of the box with something fantastic, you are more likely to impress them.

EXERCISE ONE

Take any song you've written with which you're having trouble, cover the first verse with your hand and check to see what would happen if you started with the *second* verse. You may discover that it expresses what you *really* wanted to say. Often, songwriters leave in the first verse just because it rhymes or because they didn't want to rewrite it since it went so well with the music. If this is the case with your song, replace the first verse with the second, write a new second verse, and you're home free.

EXERCISE TWO

Suppose you have to send a telegram to someone in Afghanistan. Pretend it costs $100 per word and all you have, now and forever, is $1000. And you can't send it COD. Write your telegram, telling the whole story in ten words. If it takes eleven or thirteen, keep rewriting until you're down to ten. If you can't reduce the word count, write another telegram about something else, and see if that works.

Now assume that the developments creating the need for the first telegram have changed. You need to send a second missive, also ten words long, detailing either a new situation or change in plans. Write that now.

The most obvious message would be one concerning the arrival of a plane: "arriving London Heathrow TWA flight 300, June 2, meet me." But suppose, for example, the plane is sky-jacked. The second telegram might read: "Unscheduled stop in Syria. London arrival delayed. Call French Embassy."

Try and make each telegram a verse of a song. And the next time you sit down to write a verse, see if you can reduce it to ten words or less first, to get the basic "story points" down. Then embellish them to fit your melody.

EXERCISE THREE

Now that you've sent a telegram to someone far away, let's write one home. Pretend you have only ten words to notify your spouse you're leaving, taking the kids, and going to Monaco. For the follow-up telegram, or second verse, you've changed your mind and want to come back. But your spouse's response telegram says it's too late, the blonde work-out instructor from the Boom Boom Saloon just moved in.

CHAPTER FIVE

The Impact of Images

The best lyrics, and the ones that are easiest to remember, are the ones expressing feelings through clear and fresh *images*. Now that you've seen how important it is to begin a lyric with strong opening lines, let's explore how the use of vivid imagery can keep this high level of writing consistent throughout your song.

Take Tracy Chapman's first album as an example. Her lyrics graphically and colorfully described the experience of being a street person and living in shelters. She wasn't simply saying, like everyone else was, that something should be done about the homeless in America. Listening to her album, I saw all her images clearly: a young woman working as a cashier, her dreams of riding off in a fast car, the neighbors' screams, and the ambulances wailing every night. I "lived" the life she described, and got much more involved in it than if she'd simply written "life's tough." I could *see* the tired checker's blue polyester smock and name tag. I could *see* the crowded, dismal shelter, with acres of cots. And I could *see* the neighbors in a tenement pounding on the ceiling, as the ambulance's flashing red light pulled up. It was devastating. It was terrific. It was startlingly *visual*.

Each picture word you use suggests many other images that the listener automatically associates with the first image. If you use the word "zoo" in a lyric, for example, we might imagine lions, tigers, bears, elephants, and so on, even though the only word actually used in the song was "zoo." Isn't it interesting how a three-letter, one-syllable word can create so many visual pictures?

In the hit "Twenty Years Ago" written by Christopher Spriggs, Wood Newton, Daniel Tyler, and Michael Noble, Kenny Rogers sang a visually rich lyric about going back to his home town. He discovers that the old movie theater where he and his childhood buddies went every Friday night has been closed. This image creates the picture of a crumbling cinema on Main Street, all boarded up. We can feel the sadness and share the loss through this image.

As the lyric continues, the singer passes Mr. Johnson's hardware store—not just any hardware store—but *Mr. Johnson's* hardware store. This specificity makes the image much more personal, and suggests that the singer had a relationship with the man. That relationship is personalized further when Rogers sings about Joe Johnson, an old buddy whom no one realized wouldn't make it back from "the war in '64"—Vietnam. Think of how that phrase evokes an onslaught of war images from that divisive time. Every visual word in the lyric stimulates another emotional response, bringing us deeper into the song and holding us there. As unusual as it may be, this is a love song— between the singer and his irretrievable past.

I know many of this country's best songwriters and hear a lot of great tunes, but the ones that dazzle me are those with memorable, *unpredictable* melodies, accompanied by lyrics that surprise me because they use vocabulary and imagery that's never been used in a song. There are words in our language today that didn't exist five or ten years ago, and our song lyrics should include these words. "Microchip," "turbo," "mail merge," and "Iranscam" don't appear to be the stuff of which love songs are made, but I have one client who wrote a lyric about feeling love that was so special, she wanted to freeze the moment and pop it in the microwave. Later, if she was ever lonely, she could defrost it and feel the feelings all over again. I think this is a world-class idea. We all know what microwave ovens look like, so we can visualize her as she reheats her love. Many of us own microwave ovens ourselves, and therefore the image resonates for us. The vocabulary is fresh, so the lyric works.

"Mail merge" could be a pun—*male* merge. You could say you've been stuck at your computer terminal all day in a cookie crumb-covered, tattered sweat suit, but now that the sunset's filling your window, you want to change the program, take a hot, slow shower, get dressed up in some nasty, new, black lingerie, head out into the night and do a little "male merging" of a different kind. With your man, you'll create a new program, new energy sources, and operate on your own power system.

You might think a political dilemma like "Iranscam" wouldn't work in a love song. Wrong. You could sing about how much you trusted your lover, and then when he/she cheated on you, you felt as betrayed as most Americans did after discovering that our officials made an arms deal with Iran.

If I asked you to write a love song using the Valdez oil spill, your initial reaction might be that it absolutely wouldn't work. But what if you wrote about the way the love of your life told you a teeny white lie, and tarnished your trust to the same extent Alaska was blackened by the tanker hitting an iceberg.

One evening when I'd just finished my first book that had taken six months of sixteen-hour days to complete, the man in my life was stuck in a snowbound airport and couldn't be with me to help celebrate. All my friends were busy and I wanted to party. When my boyfriend called again later that night, I told him I felt like a "showroom-new Ferrari that was up on blocks." How's that for describing frustration in a new way? And, used in the context of missing someone, it certainly could work in a love song. And it did.

The key to writing original lyrics is taking all the new words that have become part of our experience and using them in our songs. The best way to be sure your songs are heard is to freshen up your vocabulary by incorporating interesting visual imagery into every line of your lyrics.

Please remember that the purpose of the following exercises is to spark ideas and to give you practice using new writing tools, not necessarily to create hits this time out.

EXERCISE ONE

List your daily adventures in a journal each night for a week before you go to sleep. Be as specific as you can.

Go through your journal after a week with a red pen, circling all the new words you've never used before in a song. Try to incorporate these words into your writing.

EXERCISE TWO

List ten places you've explored for new images and ideas, such as reading magazines (the ones having nothing to do with music work best), or eavesdropping at an after-school teen hang-out, listening to a radio talk show, or visiting a local museum.

EXERCISE THREE

If you're still stumped for new subject matter, ask yourself what activities have you never even contemplated before. Make a list. Have you thought of working with abused children? Have you thought about installing solar heat? Going to a fire-walking party? Running for the Senate? Having an AIDS test? A home pregnancy test? All these new adventures are fertile areas in which to find new experiences and images.

EXERCISE FOUR

Make a list of every high-tech item you've bought or craved in the past two years. Some of the ones that come to mind immediately are the compact disc player (or just CD), the FAX machine, a food processor (Cuisinart is a great word because there are so many surprise rhymes with "art"), VCR, (another good rhyming word that hasn't been overused, yet), answering machine, direct dialer, cellular car phone, speaker phone. All this vocabulary is new to songs. It's fresh. It's hip. By using it, you'll find yourself with delicious new things to say in your lyrics.

EXERCISE FIVE

Read the newspaper every day. Cover to cover. Even if you're penniless, read the business section. And even if you're a klutz, read the sports pages. List three stories each day for a week that gave you something new to think about, like the Time/Warner/Paramount takeover battle, Chris Evert retiring, or the Detroit Pistons trampling the Lakers four straight in the NBA playoffs.

EXERCISE SIX

Flip open your dictionary, drop your index finger down on the first picture noun (sofa, typewriter) or proper noun (Maria, Nova Scotia) you find *that you've never used in a song.* Write down that word and find four more the same way, but in a different part of the dictionary, so not all of your words begin with the same letter. Then, repeating the process, find five visual or action adjectives you've also never used before in one of your songs, but that are realistic possibilities. Don't use any nouns or adjectives that have to do with music.

Match each noun with each adjective. That'll give you twenty-five pairs of words. Some of the word combinations will startle you. That's what they're supposed to do. Do this exercise with a big dictionary, not one of those $2.99 portable jobs. You need some *real* words here, which is why you're doing the exercise in the first place.

While this exercise is designed to simply spark ideas, Dave Wilcox, one of my clients, found the phrase "lukewarm Perrier" this way. It inspired a terrific song of the same name about a guy who was waiting endlessly for his lady at an Italian restaurant. Because he was broke, he nursed the same glass of Perrier all night while he waited.

This song could've been the same old "I-love-you-but-you-don't-love-me-anymore" song. But because the title was so unique, and because a love story was created around this sad glass of Perrier, it sounded brand new. We used to sing only about beer, whiskey, or wine. Now, with so many of us being health conscious, it's perfectly believable for a noun like Perrier to appear in a popular song. But until my client used it, I'd never heard it in one.

I recommend you do this dictionary exercise every morning before you begin your day. If you have to get up and jump right into your day job, I suggest you set your alarm five minutes earlier so you can do this exercise first thing. I guarantee if you start off the morning with new words and ideas filling your imagination, it will have a positive, domino affect on your entire day.

CHAPTER SIX

Creating Your Own Similes and Metaphors

One of the best ways to create original images with your new vocabulary is through the use of similes and metaphors. In case you were asleep the week you were supposed to learn this in English class, a simile is a comparison that begins with "like" or "as." Two examples: "I need you *like* peanut butter needs jelly"; "I want you as much *as* a ticket to Wimbledon." A metaphor is a comparison without "like" or "as": "She was bull-in-a-china-shop angry"; "he was an oak tree even while his world collapsed around him."

When we write, we use comparisons to strengthen and color our statements. When in the heat of writing many songwriters have trouble finding an original comparison, so they tend to settle for clichés.

This next exercise will eliminate that problem. Every time you think of a comparison with either "like" or "as" that strikes you as original, write it down. This way, you're creating a resource file for yourself, so the next time you're writing and need something fresh, all you have to do is turn to your comparison pages.

If you think your mind doesn't work this way, and are afraid you'll never come up with anything new, let me assure you that similes and metaphors are lurking everywhere. Last summer, I was written-out and needed a vacation. I got into my car and headed for Yosemite, the most beautiful place in California—if not the whole country. I couldn't get there in one day, so I had to stop in Fresno, where it was 110 degrees and one long, ugly, B-flat, shopping mall after another. I'm sure there are some nice people, good restaurants, and lovely hotels in that city, but I sure didn't find them. Instead, I was welcomed by perspiring cranks, greasy take-out food, and a Worst Western motel with a lumpy bed—a far cry from Yosemite, the natural, magnificent, setting in which I'd planned to spend the night. It felt like I was doing time, instead of taking time off.

But when I left at dawn the next day, and the spectacular foothills of Yosemite welcomed me, I opened the sunroof and smiled, realizing that sometimes you have to go through the Fresnos to get to the Yosemites. My friends, if you can find a metaphor in Fresno, you can find one anywhere.

EXERCISE ONE—SIMILES

Keeping in mind the emotions we use most frequently in songs, I've created headings under which you can make your own comparison lists. It would be a good idea to devote one page in a spiral notebook for each emotion.

As happy as: _____
Example: a hobo with a twenty-dollar bill.

As lonely as: _____
Example: a widow on her wedding anniversary.

As frightened as: _____
Example: a mother whose toddler is missing.

As optimistic as: _____
Example: a farmer who plants his crop during a drought.

As deserted as: _____
Example: a tennis court in the rain.

As loved as: _____
Example: a minute-old baby in his mother's arms.

As desperate as: _____
Example: a bandit, out of ammunition, surrounded by the posse.

As beautiful as: _____
Example: a Yosemite spring sunrise.

As smelly as: _____
Example: a trash bin full of week-old halibut.

As fast as: _____
Example: a Cuisinart purées.

As soft as: _____
Example: a cashmere cloud.

As improbable as: _____
Example: Gorbachev running for mayor of Malibu.

EXERCISE TWO—METAPHORS

Now try filling a page for each heading with metaphors. Here's one example: "My office is a mess—it's Armenia up here." Make a list of your own original metaphors that describe: Happiness, loneliness, being frightened, optimism, being deserted, being loved, desperation, beauty, a smelly odor, being easy, softness, an improbability.

Every time you come up with a new idea for another simile or metaphor, be sure to write it down in your notebook. Some of you are happier with yellow legal pads or the backs of envelopes. They terrify me, because the pages can blow away. But I'd be willing to negotiate this with you. How about this for our deal: scribble the idea down on anything that's handy—even the mirror or the wall, but please transfer it later into a ring-bound notebook.

When a good idea comes to you, you should treasure it. If you don't write it down and keep it somewhere safe, you could lose it, and it'll never come back to you. What's worse, it could get insulted and pop into some more appreciative writer's mind.

CHAPTER SEVEN

Rhyming

The rhymes in a lyric help make it cohesive and "sing-along-able." They also make the words easier to remember. Songs are nursery rhymes for adults, so they should be as easy to recall and sing back as "Baa Baa Black Sheep" and "Jack and Jill." And because the lyrics will be put to music, rhyming adds musicality to otherwise ordinary speech.

The most obvious place to rhyme a song is at the end of the line:

> I dressed in light blue
> So did you

Please note that while these two lines rhyme at the end of the line, the syllable count is different in each line. I did that on purpose. Many writers mistakenly believe everything has to be symmetrical. It doesn't. Varying the length of lines just adds more surprises.

As quick review, "you" and "blue" are single rhymes. "Early" and "squirelly" are double rhymes. "Go away" and "flow today" are triple rhymes.

The trouble with putting a rhyme at the end of symmetrical lines is that you continually signal where the listener should expect to hear the next rhyme sound. Since your job is to keep your audience surprised, learning to rhyme in *unexpected places* is an important skill to master. That's where internal rhymes come in.

Internal rhymes appear *inside* the lines, not at the end. They are surprising, sophisticated, and indicate a higher quality of writing. They will make your writing more interesting and intricate. And if you've been writing lyrics for a long time, you know you have to keep challenging yourself or you'll go stale.

There are two other ways of making music with your words—assonance and alliteration. If you remember, assonance is the repetition of the same vowel sound and alliteration is the repeated use of the same consonant sound.

Stephen Sondheim (*West Side Story*, *Sunday in the Park with George*) has obviously mastered the application of assonance and internal rhymes. His song "Send in the Clowns," begins: "Isn't it rich."

There are three short "i" sounds right off the bat in the first four syllables of the song. This assonance lends a subtle structure to the song immediately. Later in the same song, Sondheim writes: "Losing my timing this late in my career." The long "i" sound in "my" and "timing" creates a wonderfully cohesive glue in his lyric.

An example of an internal rhyme, and one I made up is:

We can be friends
And mend our feelings
Can't we?

There is both assonance and internal rhyme at work here: the long "e" sound in "we," "be," and "feelings," and the "end" sound in "friends" and "mend." This latter rhyme isn't perfect, but by embedding it in a line you avoid the embarrassment of "bastard" rhyming. This would've occurred if you'd tried to pass off "friends" and "mend" as an exact match. "Mend" rhymes with "friend," but with the "s" on the latter, the rhyme becomes imperfect and would look sloppy on the end of a line.

I usually urge my clients never to use "love" at the end of a line that needs a rhyme, because their choices of rhyming words are severely limited to "above," "glove," "of," and "shove." Oh, and maybe "turtle dove," if you were alive and talking during the '30s. But since we don't find "turtle doves" in our contemporary, colloquial speech, they shouldn't show up in our songs, either. Leikin's Second Law is "sing it the way you say it," and if you don't say "turtle dove," don't sing it.

However, if you use a rhyme with "love" internally, it works better. A good example is in the song "I'd Rather Leave While I'm in Love" by Peter Allen and Carol Sager:

> I'd rather <u>leave</u> while I'm in l<u>o</u>ve
> While I still bel<u>ieve</u> in the m<u>ea</u>ning <u>o</u>f the word . . .

There are two rhyming sounds at work within the above lines. The "love" sound, plus the long "e" sound. In this way the writers have a chance to really say something, instead of being boxed in and limited by the rhymes. They also use alliteration to advantage. This is the repetition of the consonant sounds in "while," "still," "believe."

Perhaps one of the best examples of internal rhyme is the first line of the song "I've Got a Name," by Norman Gimbel and Charlie Fox: "Like the p<u>ine</u> trees l<u>ine</u>ing the w<u>ind</u>ing road." See how all those "ine" rhymes work together?

Sometimes, through the clever use of assonance, you can create the illusion of rhyme:

> If N<u>o</u>tre Dame bl<u>o</u>ws it and the Tr<u>o</u>jan's win
> It's <u>a</u> red and g<u>o</u>ld R<u>o</u>se B<u>o</u>wl we'll see

I could've said "If Notre Dame dies and USC wins" but then I'd miss two of my long "o" sounds. Besides, what I *did* write says the same thing. More subtly, the <u>i</u> sound in "win" and in "it's" are also assonant. Further, I could have used "maroon" instead of "red," but the alliteration of the "r" sound adds a nice cohesiveness to the lyric. If it just rhymed at the end of the line the lyric wouldn't be as surprising or original.

There is another pay-off for the skillful use of assonance, alliteration, and internal rhyme—you get to employ all those words that don't rhyme with anything or that have so few rhymes you never put them in a lyric. The "or" sound in "orange" works well and unexpectedly with the same sound in "storm," which is usually only cliché-rhymed with "warm." So see how many ways you can make music with your words now? Here's one more example:

The storm warning on the orange radio
Was normally broadcast all morning

EXERCISE ONE

Open your dictionary at random. Drop your finger on the page, and write down the word it lands on. Without using a rhyming dictionary, list ten words that rhyme internally with the first word you found. The reason I suggest you *not* use the rhyming dictionary is I want you to learn to rhyme without a crutch. When I'm looking for a rhyme I start at the beginning of the alphabet and go through all twenty-six letters several times in my head, each time with different consonants, until I find the word I want. If you relied on a rhyming dictionary, you could settle for a word that rhymes but that doesn't say what you mean. Another of Leikin's Laws is that it's more important to say what you mean than to make something meaningless rhyme. Do this exercise every day for a week.

EXERCISE TWO

The diagrams on p. 45 contain squares, circles, and triangles. Each shape represents a different rhyme or vowel sound. The numbers between the shapes are the number of syllables I want you to put between each sound. Fill them in, choosing a different rhyme or sound for each shape, and please, don't worry about the content this time through. It doesn't have to make sense. It just has to have assonance and rhyme internally.

Diagram One

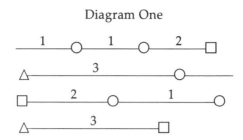

Diagram Two

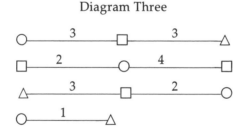

Diagram Three

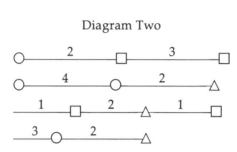

Diagram Four

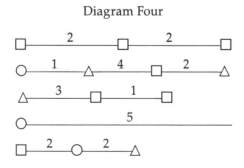

Now choose one of these patterns and write a song about a strawberry shoe, a singing Toyota, or any other bit of whimsy that pops into your head, trying to keep the assonance and internal rhymes in each line. If you have to eliminate a few of of the rhymes for the sake of articulation as you go, fine. The triangles, squares, and circles are simply meant to be guidelines for you.

EXERCISE THREE

Make up a diagram of your own, and fill in the blanks. Whenever you find yourself with five minutes free, come back to this exercise, altering the rhyme sounds and the placement slots slightly.

Try to do one diagram per day for a week, substituting different sounds each time. Try one diagram with only different alliterative sounds, and the next day try filling in the blanks with only assonant vowels. By the end of the week, you will have had a lot of practice, and will be much more comfortable with the concept of making your lyrics sing on their own.

The best songs don't *just* rhyme internally or at the end of the line. These lyrics utilize a combination of all the poet's tools. When you've incorporated these techniques into your writing process, you will be in top form.

CHAPTER EIGHT

The Evolution of a Song

I feel it would be helpful to see how some songs my clients wrote evolved from their first to final drafts. These examples demonstrate how the art of songwriting is a process and rarely a single gust of inspiration.

DONUT DAYS

When I heard Dannie La Russo's mid-tempo, light rock tune for the first time, I thought there were some fabulous things in it and urged my client to keep working on it. She did. With her permission, I'm including the first and the final drafts, with my comments.

DONUT DAYS: First draft

VERSE
Times once hard seem easy now
When I look back on them
I still see us starting out
Lord it was rough, but it was simpler

We had certain freedoms there
With ends never meeting
That nowadays we wouldn't dare
Now we just remember

When struggle was a best friend
Sometimes I wish that life would send us:

CHORUS
Back to the days of donuts and coffee in the car
Back when one day soon seemed like someday off so far
Back to the days of talkin' 'bout who we're gonna be
Back when the grown-up world seemed no place for us to be

VERSE
Dog and us sleepin' on the floor
Always wakin' hungry
So we'd all drive down to the store
Buy us something sweet and pleasing

All those Sundays 9 P.M.
Took a drive and took
A load off Monday's garbagemen
God you appreciate the things you find

When struggle is your best friend
Sometimes I wish that life would send us:

(REPEAT FIRST CHORUS)

BRIDGE
Baby hey what do ya say
Let's go get something sugar frosted
If we can't find joy let's go lookin' boy
'Cause that don't mean we lost it
That don't mean we lost it
I think we could find it
If we go:

CHORUS
Back for a day of donuts and coffee in the car
Back 'cause one day soon isn't someday off too far
Back for a day of talkin' 'bout who we've come to be
Back 'cause the grown-up world seems the place we got
     to be

VERSE
Sometimes I stare out at the lawn
Where the old dog lays
And feel the chill of ancient dawns
When we greeted life with hunger

When struggle was our best friend
Sometimes I wish that life would send us:

(REPEAT SECOND CHORUS)

COMMENTS

I am convinced Dannie will be the Joni Mitchell of the '90s. She's articulate, visual, intelligent, original, melodic, and a perfectionist. She has exceptionally high standards for herself, and so I know how far to push her. In this song, I loved the title. First, the alliteration was appealing, and made the title easy to remember. Second, I'd heard lots of songs about the good old days when we were broke, but I hadn't heard any expressed just this way. It's always acceptable to write about a subject that's been dealt with before—as long as you have a new approach.

However, I felt Dannie could get to what the song was about quicker and more visually. The first two verses in this draft were just too general and wishy-washy, although I did love the walk-up section which leads to the chorus, because of the surprising rhythmic change. So I asked Dannie to rewrite the first verse, making the lyrics more visual and direct. We needed an immediate picture that would show us what her song was about in the first few lines.

Also, I didn't believe that the story in this draft progressed as well as it should, and I asked Dannie to embellish it with specific incidents so the song would be about more than just being poor and hungry. I loved the fact that she named her song dog, "Dog," but I felt there were other story points that she could include in order to make her narrative more interesting. For example, the image of the two characters in this song going shopping in trash bins before the garbagemen got there is extremely sharp. How's that for a romantic image of poverty?

As for the chorus, I felt there could be a stronger line than the second one, "when someday soon seemed like someday off so far." Granted, she was restricted by the "ar" rhyme of "car," but I knew if she dug deep enough she could come up with a picture that would have more impact.

Even though this song has a fabulous melody and a chorus hook that won't quit, I still felt it was too long. I suggested that Dannie omit the last verse, so it would be a verse/chorus, verse/chorus, bridge/chorus/chorus song.

There are often good things we have to take out of songs to make room for something that works better with the *whole* song. A good line that shows off a little but doesn't help the tune should be cut. I suggested Dannie think of the analogy of a basketball team. When the team is really playing as a team, they win. But if the one of the players hogs the ball at everyone's expense, the team loses.

One thing I admired in Dannie's writing is that she doesn't try to make everything rhyme. If you look back at the verses, you'll see she uses her rhymes sparingly, so she gets to say what she wants to say without the restrictions of rhymes. In the walk-up section, she uses a good, unexpected internal rhyme—the "en" sound in "friend" and "send."

Dannie was very open to making the changes I suggested. Several drafts later, the final one evolved.

DONUT DAYS by Dannie La Russo: Final Draft

VERSE
Remember sittin' by the road
Just dunkin' our donuts

Our beat-up pick up gettin' towed
We shrugged and said "that's livin'"

Those were times we couldn't care
If ends weren't meeting
Nowadays we'd never dare
Now we just remember

When struggle was a best friend
Sometimes I wish that life would send us:

CHORUS
Back to the days of donuts and coffee in the car
Back to saying grace for an apple and a peanut butter jar
Back to the days of talkin' 'bout who we're gonna be
Back 'cause the grown-up world seemed no place for us
    to be

VERSE
One day you asked and I said yes
So we drove to the thrift store
And you bought me that fancy dress
And we stole flowers from a garden

Honeymoon Sunday nine PM
Took a drive and took
A load off Monday's garbagemen
God we were grateful for the junk we found

When struggle was our best friend
Sometimes I wish that life would send us

(REPEAT FIRST CHORUS)

BRIDGE
Baby hey what do ya say
Let's go get something sugar frosted
If we can't find joy let's go lookin' boy
'Cause that don't mean we lost it

That don't mean we lost it
I think we could find it
If we go:

CHORUS
Back for a day of donuts and coffee in the car
Back to say our grace for an apple and a peanut butter jar
Back for a day of talkin' bout who we've come to be
Back 'cause the grown-up world is the place we got to be

© 1989 Dannie La Russo.

I loved the new picture of these two penniless kids sitting on a curb watching their poor vehicle being hauled away by a tow truck. It brought back the years I drove a beat-up, faded VW with a leaky sun roof. Everybody romanticizes being poor when we're not poor anymore so I felt that creating this image of the old truck being towed away was one everybody could relate to in a wistful, positive way. It's a songwriter's job to bring the audience into his/her song, and I felt Dannie really did a terrific job of rewriting this verse.

In the chorus, I got goose-bumps from the line "Back to saying grace for an apple and a peanut butter jar." You can *see* the sad little apple and the almost-empty peanut butter jar, but the part that really got me in this line was giving *thanks* for having that meager meal. Dannie's new line added a tremendous richness to her song that was missing in the earlier draft.

In the new second verse the story made a progression. He proposed, she accepted, and they went shopping for a wedding gown at a thrift store and then stole flowers from a stranger's garden for the bride's bouquet. I loved the tradition of the wedding gown juxtaposed with the rebelliousness of stealing flowers. Putting opposite images and ideas together give a song a wonderful texture and substance. I am not shy about saying what I feel, and I fought hard to convince Dannie to substitute the phrase "bridal" dress for "fancy dress." But it's Dannie's song and in the end, she has the final say.

When Dannie first came to me, she had armfuls of unfinished songs. Now, she has learned how to develop the earlier drafts of her songs, so that they are becoming finished drafts sooner. Through our meetings, she's learned to be a good editor and to get to what she wants to say as quickly, and as emotionally and visually as possible.

SILVER PROMISES

I was very flattered when Larry Livingston, the Dean of Music at the University of Southern California, referred Anita Kruse to me. Not only is Anita a gifted singer/songwriter, but she's a wonderful person, and over the months we've worked together has become my friend as well as my client.

When we had our initial consultation, I was surprised to find that Anita was very unsure about herself and her considerable singing and songwriting talents. Part of her insecurity could have stemmed from her classical background. Moreover, she is married to Larry Rachleff, a very successful musical conductor who is in great demand all over the world. Larry has been very supportive of Anita's songwriting dreams—he just couldn't help her because he didn't know the pop marketplace or the qualities that make a pop tune *great*. But I do, and I'd like to share the process by which one of Anita's songs evolved to become a potentially big hit.

SILVER PROMISES: First Draft

VERSE
A springtime wedding
With an ocean view
Everything tied in silver bows
And perfectly timed I do's
Music by Handel
Sunset by God
And every vow engraved
With a preacher's nod

CHORUS
We made silver promises
That April by the sea
You said you'd spend a lifetime
In love with me
We made silver promises
Our lives had just begun
Now every one, every one
Has come undone

VERSE
So you tell me
You're going away
You're in love with someone else
And there's nothing I can say
I'm sure I've lost you
Cause it's empty in your eyes
But I know my heart
Will never cut the ties

CHORUS
We made silver promises
That April by the sea
You said you'd spend a lifetime
In love with me
We made silver promises
Our lives had just begun
Now every one, every one
Has come undone.

I loved some of the imagery in this first draft. I could easily picture the "springtime wedding" overlooking the ocean, with big silver bows around the flowers, and beaming bridesmaids, the ever-present photographers, and a mouthwatering banquet feast. I especially loved the lines "Music by Handel/Sunset by God." Written by someone who didn't have Anita's talent, this first verse could have seemed clichéd. Instead, I found it brilliantly original.

The chorus started off with a nice change in rhythm from the verse's meter, providing that all-important "hook." Even so, I didn't feel the chorus lyric ended as well as it could. I certainly write my share of sad songs, but I felt this one might work better if it concluded with perhaps a small promise of hope. I suggested that Anita could fill the second verse with pictures of how the two lovers in the song might rekindle their feelings for one another.

When I read her rewrite, it was clear that this second draft was a big improvement.

SILVER PROMISES: Second Draft

VERSE
A springtime wedding
With an ocean view
Everything tied in silver bows
And perfectly timed I do's
Music by Handel
Sunset by God
And every vow engraved
With a preacher's nod

CHORUS
We made silver promises
That April by the sea
You said you'd spend a lifetime
In love with me
Now our silver promises
Have tarnished in the wind
So you and I, you and I
Must pull them in

VERSE
We'll spend the day together
And wander in the park
Share a midnight meal by candlelight
And ice cream in the dark

We'll dance without music
And dream without sleep
And remember we have
Promises to keep

CHORUS
We made silver promises
That April by the sea
You said you'd spend a lifetime
In love with me
Now our silver promises
Have tarnished in the wind
So you and I, you and I
Must pull them in.

In this version, I felt Anita's rewritten chorus was much closer to what it should be, but it still wasn't quite right. I had a problem with the near rhymes: "wind" and "in" don't rhyme perfectly. Nobody will ever send you to prison for using them as rhyming words, but the trouble was that Anita was writing around the problem, not addressing it directly. When two people are having a rocky relationship they don't see their problems as something they have to "pull in." So the language of this line felt a little strained and unnatural to me. But the thought behind the words was closer in spirit to what I felt Anita should shoot for.

I was very pleased with the progress she'd made from the first draft. While the new second verse had come a long way from the first, I felt "midnight meal by candlelight" was too general, and suggested Anita be more specific about what that meal consisted of. I also felt it would be more romantic if the food wasn't "sensible" or "normal," and was instead something indulgent and a little unexpected. I really liked the second half of this verse, however, and felt this song was very close to having everything it needed to become a hit. I urged on one more rewrite and I think Anita accomplished every songwriter's goal: she made a good song, a hit song.

SILVER PROMISES by Anita Kruse: Final Draft

VERSE
A springtime wedding
With an ocean view
Everything tied with silver bows
And perfectly timed I do's
Music by Handel
Sunset by God
And every vow engraved
With a preacher's nod

CHORUS
We made silver promises
That April by the sea
You said you'd spend a lifetime
In love with me
But our silver promises
Have tarnished in the wind
God I hope we can make them
Shine again

VERSE
Let's wake up late tomorrow
And wander in the park
Share ice cream cones by candlelight
And chocolate in the dark
Let's dance without music
And dream without sleep
And remember we have
Promises to keep

CHORUS
We made silver promises
That April by the sea
You said you'd spend a lifetime
In love with me
But our silver promises

Have tarnished in the wind
God I hope we can make them
Shine again

BRIDGE
Why leave our futures to the wind and weather
When all we need is time together . . .

CHORUS
We made silver promises
That April by the sea
You said you'd spend a lifetime
In love with me
But our silver promises
Have tarnished in the wind
God I hope we can make them
Shine again.

© 1990 Anita Kruse

In this final draft, Anita took my suggestion and made the end of the chorus more conversational, and, I feel, more real. We *would* say to one another what she wrote in the final line: "God I hope that we can make them shine again." I was also pleased that she took my recommendation and used the words "tarnish" and "shine" to balance each other.

I loved the romantic pictures she created in the second verse. I've heard a lot of songs in my lifetime, but I've never heard one that sang about "ice cream cones by candlelight." A less talented writer might have settled for wine with the candles, which is a cliché. "Chocolate in the dark" is another arrestingly original image, and I was proud that Anita had taken my suggestion to dig a little deeper and tell me something new.

Since singing the song all the way through to this point only took two minutes, I advised Anita to insert a bridge after the second chorus. The one she wrote has a nice, positive, "we-can-and-will-work-this-out" attitude, lending the song a hopeful feeling.

As long as you, the songwriter, follow Dannie or Anita's example and willingly make the changes that are best for your song, you should be able to transform medium lyrics into marvelous ones.

It is much easier to be tough on other writers' work than on your own. So you don't think I'm only hard on other songwriters, I'm including one of my songs and will show you how it evolved.

IN MY NEXT LIFETIME: First Draft

VERSE
Timing is everything
I'm sad to say
I really love you
Even so I'm leaving today
'Cause you made a life
With somebody else
I won't stand in your way

CHORUS
But in my next lifetime
We'll be together
When it's the right time
We'll have it all

VERSE
All that I'm living for
Is to love you again
So I know we'll meet someday
On the way though I don't know when
So I won't say goodbye
It's only so long
Take care my love 'til then

CHORUS
In my next lifetime
We'll be together

Knowing you'll love me
Will keep me going
When it's the right time
We'll find each other
In my next lifetime
We'll have it all

BRIDGE
If you believe in this as strongly as I do
Our thoughts will join hands and lead me back to you

(REPEAT SECOND CHORUS)

I was totally in love with the melody, which came to me whole in my sleep. This was amazing, since I hadn't written a song in six years. So I had good reason to want to make this song as close to perfect as I could.

Although I liked the first verse, the second verse didn't feel emotional enough. This song was about a very real and passionate relationship I'd had, tangled up with the same man for eleven years. We couldn't stay away from each other, but finally we broke up. Because I cry easily I felt I should be in tears when I sang the second verse. And I wasn't. So I tried a new second verse:

All that I'm living for
Is to love you again
So I know we'll meet someday
On the way though I don't know when
We'll travel the world
We'll dance in the rain
Take care my love 'til then

While I liked the second half of this verse because of the pictures and the romantic fantasy of it, it still didn't make me cry. The melody cried—I knew the lyric had to as well.

I was stuck for six weeks, and since it was making me crazy, I decided to go on a vacation, thinking the change of scene might spark my muse. Besides, my ex-boyfriend's daughter was getting married, and he was totally absorbed in those plans and not paying any attention to missing me. I thought he and I should've been planning our own wedding, but we'd already broken up.

Anyhow, off I went to Peru, and the third day out, I got a terrible altitude headache at 13,000 feet. I had to be evacuated to sea level immediately, leaving the tour and all my adventurous new friends. It was very sad. Since I couldn't get a direct flight and had to spend the night all by myself in Lima, I went into the hotel bar to kill some time, and found an old upright piano. I sat down at the keyboard, feeling alone and abandoned, and started playing my melody. That's when the second verse came to me:

> I see our wedding day
> And our children too
> The moonlight and Christmases
> Of my dreams are gonna come true
> So I won't say goodbye
> It's only so long
> 'Cause I'll be seeing you

Since I couldn't sing this verse without bursting into tears, I knew I had written a good one. When a cute British backpacker in the bar slipped a twenty-dollar bill into my empty Perrier glass, I knew the song had to be a hit, especially considering my meek little flat singing voice.

While the original bridge was articulate, there were no surprises from a rhythmic point of view. So I edited out some of the lyric bulk to make the rhythm more interesting. Eventually, I said almost what I wanted to say originally.

IN MY NEXT LIFETIME by Molly-Ann Leikin: Final Draft

VERSE
Timing is everything
I'm sad to say
I really love you

Even so I'm leaving today
'Cause you made a life
With somebody else
I won't stand in your way

CHORUS
But in my next lifetime
We'll be together
When it's the right time
We'll have it all

VERSE
I see our wedding day
And our children too
The moonlight and Christmases
Of my dreams are gonna come true
So I won't say goodbye
It's only so long
'Cause I'll be seeing you

CHORUS
In my next lifetime
We'll be together
Knowing you'll love me
Will keep me going
When it's the right time
We'll find each other
In my next lifetime
We'll have it all

BRIDGE
If you believe in this
Believe as strong as I do
Our thoughts'll bring me back to you

(REPEAT SECOND CHORUS)

© 1989 Scc Rcc Songs

With this final draft I felt that I said something nobody else had said quite this way before in a song. I was also very pleased with the internal structure of sounds. I could have said "even so, I'm going away" but "leaving today" extended the "e" sound in "even." I also changed "you have a life with somebody else" to "you made a life," extending the assonance in the words "say," "day," and "way." I substituted "I can't stand in your way" with "I won't stand in your way," since the two "w's" make it alliterative.

At first glance, it may seem that the chorus doesn't rhyme at all. If you think about it, what could you rhyme with "together" that isn't predictable? "Forever"? So I chose not to rhyme it in the expected places. The long "i" sound in "lifetime" echoes in "right time." And in the double chorus, "knowing" rhymes with "going," again in a surprise place. And the long "i" sound in "right time" repeats in "find."

This song took the longest to complete of any lyric I've ever written. But I'm prouder of it than of any of my hits to date. So what's a few months of agony and an altitude headache? A temporary inconvenience, when you consider the elation of finally getting it right.

CHAPTER NINE

How to Map Out New Song Ideas

Many of my new clients come to me extremely frustrated—they have great ideas for songs but don't know how to develop them. So I believe it might be helpful to take a new idea I had recently and show you how I turned it into a song.

Whenever I get a title, I like to map it out to make sure there really is enough material to warrant writing a whole song. That is where many of my new clients run into trouble. They rush headlong into the writing process without checking first to see if they have enough to say to fill two verses, a chorus, and a bridge. It's important to figure out what goes where before you even start to write, before you're tangled up in meter and rhyme constrictions, and are still able to *say what you mean, not just what rhymes.*

To most people in our collective radio audience, many of whom live by love songs, falling in love is considered the best thing that could happen to them. Those who aren't in love, wish they were. People in loveless relationships, wish they'd meet someone new, so the glorious high could start all over for them.

That is not news.

The song title I'm going to use as an example is "Fallout." I knew immediately it could work in any genre. It also passed what I call the "Opposites Test": words or phrases that oppose but balance each other. For instance, almost every other song I hear is about falling *in* love, but I when I got this title, it occurred to me, I hadn't heard one about falling *out*, which is the hard part.

"Fall out," is a pun, referring to both the end of a romance, and the after effects of an atomic explosion. Although we *talk* about nuclear radiation fallout all the time, I'd never heard it in a love song before.

Since I knew it was a strong title, here's how I developed it. In my notebook, I took a fresh page for each song section and wrote:

1. Here's what I want to say in the first verse:
2. Here's what I could say in the chorus:
3. Here's what the second verse will say:
4. If I have time and need a little "oomph" at the end, here's what the bridge could say:

I referred back to my old notebook to show you the way this song took shape. It may be helpful for you to study my notes in order to develop a process of your own.

What I want to say in the first verse:

Nothing's better than falling in love: feeling needed, having passion back in my life, my skin clearing up, my disposition improving 1000 percent, my happiness is contagious. I'm willing to jump into this.

What I want to say in the chorus:

I wasn't thinking about the fall out: the hard nights of loneliness, the hunger, the vulnerability, the discomfort, the possibility that it won't work and I'll be left again. It's great to relinquish control and go with it, no matter what happens.

I had forgotten 'bout the fall out
completely forgotten the other side of love
Like when you leave me and I call out
Come on back, come on back but you're gone, long
    gone

What I want to say in the second verse:

Make the verse specific to this relationship. Maybe something
like—I was happy to fluff both our pillows every morning. Now
when I do mine, I hate yours for being unused. I know it's better
if you don't come back to mess it up, but I pray you will.

Or maybe it was good being in a couple, I felt accepted by
people who are afraid to be around single women for fear we'll
steal their husbands, and my life was better than even I, with my
wild imagination, could dream up.

I don't know about radiation
but it couldn't be worse than this
I feel like someone just dropped a bomb
jolting change from the idyllic calm
and there's chaos in my life
and there's screaming
but I can't go to the red cross
they can't handle this kind of loss
emergency
no insurance
that's what you get when you sign up for love
when you line up

What I want to say in the bridge, if I need one:

In spite of the agony, if I had it to do all over again, I would.

One of the advantages of "mapping out" the lyric is you
make sure there really is enough to say to fill up a whole song, so
you don't go to all the trouble of writing a first verse and chorus,
only to find you don't have a last verse, and consequently can't
finish the song.

EXERCISE ONE

Write "Fallout," using my notes. Make it a verse/chorus song. You choose the genre. If you're undecided about which one, I'd recommend R&B.

EXERCISE TWO

Choose two titles from the list below, and map them out according to the four-part plan above. Make one a ballad and one uptempo, just to keep it interesting.

- ◆ Rock and Roll Responsibilities
- ◆ Mondays and Taxes
- ◆ Dislocated Shoulder
- ◆ I'd Love to Quit, But I Can't
- ◆ Corn Bread and Sushi

Now that you've had some experience with the mapping out process, go back and choose another title from the list above, and map out a third song. Or if you prefer, choose a title of your own. As you get ideas for each new song down the road, I recommend you map them out, too. That way, you will eliminate a lot of dead ends, and your writing will be much more productive.

CHAPTER TEN

How to Write Stronger Melodies

The first inadequacies that anyone hears in a song are in its melody. No matter whether the listener is a publisher, producer, A&R person, or gas station attendant, when people hear your song, they all hear the melody first. It isn't until they've heard the tune several times that they actually hear what the words say. So the strength of the tune is critical, because if you don't have a strong melody, nobody will listen to more than a few bars, no matter how good the lyric is.

RANGE

A contemporary pop singer with a good voice usually has a range of an octave and three notes. But not all composers use that full range in their melodies, so their music suffers. Or their songs exceed the normal range and practically nobody can sing them. Then the only person on the planet with the pipes to handle the song passes.

Even if you *do* sing your own songs and sound better than Michael Bolton or Tiffany or Madonna or Reba McEntire, I recommend you keep the normal human vocal limits in the front of your mind and write accordingly. That way, if an artist other than you wants to record one of your songs, you won't lose the record because he or she can't hit the high note.

Let's be very practical about this. If you were going to manufacture jeans, you'd do some market research to find what hip sizes and leg lengths actually fit your customers before you manufactured your product, right? Okay. You'd create clothes that fit. The same is true with melodies. Make them fit. If the range that's comfortable for a singer is an octave and three, make your sale easier by writing a song the singer wants. I've always believed in selling tomatoes to someone in the market for tomatoes. Don't offer them tofu.

From the "Trauma Center of Molly's Music Archives" I seem to remember that Tanya Tucker couldn't reach the high note in my song "Silver Wings & Golden Rings" and Frank Sinatra couldn't hit the top one in "You Set My Dreams to Music." It wasn't that these artists didn't have the chops. Quite the contrary. It was the songs' fault. Both of them were too rangey. I would've killed for either cut, but by the time I found out the reason for the passes other material had been chosen. A rewrite was impossible because of time constraints. I learned the hard way.

I keep at least three pairs of Reeboks in my closet at all times because they're so comfortable. I don't have a single pair of shoes that look gorgeous but hurt my feet. So when you write songs, create what I call "Reebok melodies"—tunes that are comfortable, sell easily, and bring repeat customers.

BUILDING A MELODY

I suggest to my clients that they use the whole octave and three in constructing their melodies, which should move up the scale as their songs progress. As they build, the tension increases in the music, and each time it does the audience is hooked again. If your melody doesn't have that tension, the hook disappears. Or if the verse is higher than the chorus, the melody usually deflates, like air hissing out of a tire.

If you trace the path of your melody line, it should move up and up, like a graph. Of course there are exceptions, because music is an art, and art is knowing what the rules are and when to break them. Many songs on the radio modulate to a new key when the chorus hook comes, but I don't recommend relying on doing that, because it signals the melody is weak and wouldn't work without the modulation. I urge you to get good at writing melodies without "tricks" first and then getting cute and clever with key changes later.

Some recent hit melodies that follow the rule of moving up the scale are "How Am I Supposed to Live Without You" by Michael Bolton, "Endless Summer Nights" and "Angelia" by Richard Marx, and "Could've Been" by Tiffany. These artists sell a lot of records, so their songs are excellent models.

TIMING

Many melodies suffer from taking too long to get to the hook. Or they don't ever get to one. A good song to study is "I'm Your Man" by Wham, in which the melody and rhythm pattern change every twelve seconds. This song was an enormous hit, but most melodies don't surprise their listeners as profoundly as this one did. A good rule of thumb is to allow about twenty-five seconds to get from the intro to the first line of the chorus. Not thirty-five seconds and not forty-five seconds. Twenty-five. And don't let your chorus exceed twenty-five seconds, either. Since the total elapsed time in a song should be two minutes and thirty seconds, this allows for two verses, two choruses, and a chorus to fade on.

SURPRISES

To me, listening to songs is like going to the movies. I want to be surprised. If I can predict what's coming up, it's boring. Your first consideration in rewriting melodies is to make sure there are surprises in your tunes. For example, if each of your verses is eight bars, try writing one with seven or nine. As the audience, we're accustomed to expecting eight. So if we hear seven or nine, that's news. That's interesting. If you aren't bar-oriented and write tunes in terms of lyric lines, instead of having a four-line verse, try one with five or three or even three and a half. This will give your melody a lot more opportunities to startle your audience and keep them interested enough to listen to what's coming next.

EDITING MELODIES

The best way to judge the strength of a melody is to put it away for a week and divert your attention to other things in the meantime. Then, when the week is up, you will, hopefully, be distanced enough from what you've created to decide whether it "flies" or needs some more work. If it doesn't work, here are some questions to ask yourself:

1. Would the hook be easier to remember if you cut down on the number of notes? Try it.
2. Would the tune be easier to remember if you vary the rhythm and not have every note come in a predictable place at a predictable time? Try it.
3. If neither of these suggestions works, could you find an alternative tune? There are endless combinations of notes so the possibilities are limitless. Don't think that because you wrote something one way it has to stay that way.
4. If you've tried all of the above and your tune still sounds predictable and boring, could you use a different rhythm or groove? I used to hate drum machines because I felt they were like drugs—once you use them, you can't do without them. But if you're stuck, and don't hear a variety of rhythms in your head, try working to a drum machine. Vary the beat and see if that sparks any new ideas. I bet it will.

I am offering you the following creative songwriting exercises, and I want you to put all your "shoulds" in a drawer and lock it. These are experiments, just for practice, so they don't "count," okay? Nobody's going to hear what you write and say, "Who does this guy think he is—President of 'Trite is Right'?" These exercises are just for practice. And, I hope, for fun.

Even if you're a lyricist who doesn't write melodies, do these musical exercises anyway. You may discover that your ear for language translates into an ability to come up with catchy tunes. Here's a story to reinforce my suggestion.

For fifteen years, all I ever wrote were lyrics. I then stopped writing songs completely for six and a half years, in favor of screenplays. In one of my scripts there was a scene where two lovers danced in the snow while one of them recited the Robert Frost poem, "Stopping by the Woods on a Snowy Evening." As I wrote the scene, I remember thinking to myself: "The composer who scores this movie will write a pretty tune to this poem."

Feeling the itch to hear the poem set to music, I started calling composers I'd worked with earlier in my career and left messages on fifty answering machines across America. But everybody I called was busy.

However, there was a melody in my head that kept waking me up in the middle of the night. I ignored it for the first week, thinking "nah, I don't write tunes, a melody of mine couldn't be any good." But since I *am* a consultant, and I do critique other writers' melodies, I hired myself and listened over and over to my cassette, trying to be objective. And I honestly thought the melody was good, even if I had written it. When I finally got up the courage to play it for some friends, I told them a client composed it, just so they wouldn't feel obligated to say they liked the tune in order to spare my feelings.

They loved it. Some of them cried. And I've never been so proud. Since then, I've written some other terrific tunes by myself. That never would've happened if I'd kept telling myself I only wrote lyrics. So if you think you just write lyrics, do the exercises anyway. There may be some music in you yet.

EXERCISE ONE

The thought of having to write a whole new melody is often intimidating to my clients. So, as an exercise, I ask them to take one line every morning—either from a newspaper headline, from a snatch of dialogue that they've overheard, or from a billboard—and set that one line to music. Here are some examples:

- How's your back?
- Did you-know-who call you?
- That's what I call a sunrise.
- Wife is a four-letter word.
- Dan Quayle makes me proud to be a Canadian.
- It's a five-five tie in the fifth set.
- Ten percent off the April sale price.
- The swans on the lawn are gone away.
- Leave the boy a big tip.

Although I usually don't write R&B songs, the first title, "How's Your Back," sounds like an R&B song to me. Three short, staccato notes. But it could also be a big ballad. Like the melody of the line "take my hand" in the song Elvis sang called "I Can't Help Falling in Love with You." (But don't use *that* melody—make up a new one.) Maybe the three notes could be a hymn, and if you're plagued with back problems, believe me, hymns are definitely in order. It could be a lullaby. Or a march. Or a jingle, selling three-speed cordless spine massagers.

For every phrase of lyric, there are endless ways to translate it into music. Not all of them will make sense or work, but try each line of lyric with four or five different melodies. Make it fun and interesting by changing the rhythm and the tempo. Don't write everything in 4/4 or in the same key. Throw in a 3/4 or a 7/8 now and then, just to keep yourself on your toes, especially if those are time signatures in which you've never written. Mix up the eighth notes, quarter notes, whole notes. And throw in some rests, too.

If you're a schooled musician, jot down the notes. If you don't write music, record everything on a cassette. Keep it rolling as you work on this exercise. You never know what you might stumble across by accident. Once you've got it on tape, you've got it forever. But if you think you don't need to tape it because you're sure you'll remember it later, kiss it goodbye.

Before you get to your instrument, say each phrase out loud a number of times to hear what the natural rhythm of the words sound like. If you learn to do this away from your instrument, you'll gain much more confidence as a composer because you'll be relying on your natural creativity rather than on an instrument, or a machine, for your ideas. And this way, you'll be able to write wherever and whenever an idea hits you— even if you don't have your instrument handy. Best of all, you can't pretend that you can't work because you forgot to pay the light bill, the power's been shut off, and your synthesizer doesn't run on batteries.

Try each phrase with different instruments. Something that sounds mundane on a guitar can come alive on a piano.

I purposely chose some phrases for the list above with internal rhymes, because those are natural places for notes to be stressed. That's also true of any line that's alliterative or assonant. I hear the line "Stab me and smile" with a pause after "me," but you may not want one or you may put it in a different place. Start creating melodies for every line of conversation you hear, every ad tag line, every sentence or sentence fragment you read, as if your life is an opera, in which all verbal communication is sung.

EXERCISE TWO

Write an eight-bar verse melody that slowly builds and moves up the scale. If you don't usually create tunes thinking in terms of bars, then write one that's four or five lyric lines long. Make sure the range of the verse doesn't exceed an octave and one, so it still leaves room for you to go higher in the chorus.

If the verse melody you decide to write for this exercise is a ballad, when you finish it, write another one that's uptempo or R&B. And if the first one you write is a dance tune, make the second a ballad. It couldn't hurt to get some practice writing in different styles.

EXERCISE THREE

For fun, I suggest you tape a three-minute, heated interchange between some household members. It could occur first thing in the morning when you're all fighting for the bathroom or the paper or the orange juice. When you've got the scene transcribed, set the dialogue to music. Don't worry about verse/chorus. Just write music for the dialogue. While you probably won't hear this song on the Grammy show this year, the exercise will make you stretch, and stretching is the best thing you can do for a creative spirit.

EXERCISE FOUR

For this exercise, you have a choice. Either set all the messages on your answering machine to music. Or compose melodies for the titles to ten "how-to" books at your local bookstore.

EXERCISE FIVE

Once I was feeling particularly creative while I was baking and started singing my recipe for sour cream cinnamon raisin coffee cake. I can't tell you that Sting cruised my condo, desperate to cut the song, but writing it sure was fun. And it made me feel like I was having a new creative experience instead of feeling trapped in my office all day, writing songs that had to have choruses.

For this assignment, set your favorite recipe to music, even if it's only bologna and cheese, ham & eggs, or pasta with peaches. For those of you who don't cook, compose a melody for the Jack in the Box drive through menu. If you think this is dumb, remember that the original title for "Easter Parade" was "Smile and Show Your Dimple" . . . .

EXERCISE SIX

Write a melody with two notes in it, but which is seven bars long. Rhythm is obviously very important in a song with so few pitches. Next, try a tune with three notes, then four, six, and eight, varying the number of bars. These melodies may not make it to the top 40, but I promise the experience will be stimulating and might lead to some other musical idea that *will* win a Grammy. I've seen some terrific songs come out of this exercise, so try it.

EXERCISE SEVEN—THE DICE GAME

When my clients are stuck and their tunes are all sounding the same, I tell them to get a pair of dice. Roll one of them once. That's the number of lines in the verse or chorus of a new melody they have to write. The next roll determines the number of different notes in each line.

I just did the exercise. My first roll was five—so my verse or chorus has five lines. My second roll was six. Therefore, my first line must have six different notes. When you're looking to compose something that's interesting and off the beaten track, try the dice game. It works.

EXERCISE EIGHT—THE DICE GAME II

Let's take the dice game one step further. Once you throw the dice and determine how many lines there are and how many notes there are in each line, roll the dice again, assigning each number a note. So, if you're in C, and roll a six, the note would be F. If you roll a twelve, the note is B.

Do three of these and see what you come up with. Keep the cassette rolling as you play. You never know what's going to come up, and if you don't record the tune, it could get insulted and go play itself on somebody else's piano.

EXERCISE NINE

Take the lyric to one of the hits you like on the radio right now and compose another melody to it. Be sure that both your rhythm and meter are different from the original song. One of my clients in Chicago wrote another melody to "That's What Friends Are For," but his rhythm and meter were identical to Burt Bacharach's, the composer of the song. You want your melody to sound original, so approach the lyric as though there isn't an existing melody or rhythm at all.

Use these exercises as a way of getting a fresh start, and then go wherever the impulse of each exercise takes you. Just promise me you won't get predictable. That's the biggest downfall of all melodies.

PART TWO

The Psychology
of Songwriting

CHAPTER ELEVEN

How to Cope with Rejection

Now that you know how to rewrite, edit, and polish your songs so they can realistically compete with the best in the marketplace, it's important to understand and overcome the psychological barriers that separate most songwriters from their success.

Rejection is the number one emotional murderer in the music business. It's devastating in any business, but especially lethal in the music industry because most songwriters create from their own experience. When their work is rejected, they feel a deep personal failure too.

The process of doing business in our business is overwhelming to most new songwriters. You pour your soul into a song, make what you think is a perfect demo, send it to fifty publishers expecting to make your fortune with it. But you discover that you are either totally ignored or sent nebulous form letters and thoughtless "nah—I passed" remarks from cold, cruel, preoccupied people running out to have lunch with writers who are hot, and thus, "worth their time."

Rejection doesn't come any tougher.

However, the longer I write, the more I'm convinced that the difference between success and failure hinges on how we handle rejection. Ours is a business of "no's," so that's the response we should expect. Even though the people who reject us are perceived as villains, we need to understand that their jobs are not to say "yes" and make us famous. Their jobs are to keep their jobs. They have to tell people "no" all day long. So if you make it okay for someone to turn you down graciously, he'll be much more likely to see you again for a potential "yes" than if you slash his tires.

One of my clients was constantly upset when someone asked her if she'd had any songs published. She'd been trying for a long time and had received a few encouraging nibbles, but hadn't had enough success to satisfy her ambitions. So questions like "Have you ever been published?" would devastate her. But I coached her to respond, "Yes, I've been published, and I've managed to have a career anyway," instead of becoming insulted by the insinuation that she was an unknown rank amateur.

That snappy answer takes her out of the position of being a victim, which is crucial, since nobody, especially in business, wants to deal with losers. We connect more readily with winners who bring us good energy. So I recommend that you have some positive responses to other people's negativity handy at all times. When someone listens to your song and tells you, "I hated that tune," thank him for his candor, tell him you understand what a hard job it is to have to say "no" to sensitive people all day, and ask him which of his other projects need material right now, because you are prolific and you're sure you can give him what he wants. That keeps the door open. The relationship stays fluid and creates another chance for you to get closer to a "yes."

I should make it very clear that while I encounter it daily, I never *condone* rudeness, hostility, stupidity, insensitivity, or any of the other brick walls we frequently confront in our music industry colleagues, no matter how famous or powerful. These character flaws abound and aren't going away. It's critical *not to personalize* them. Instead, make the commitment to keep on writing and networking in spite of everyone else's psychoses.

Each rejection we've experienced in our lives should be dealt with quickly and then discarded. Otherwise, our feelings keep building until we're an emotional powder keg. The negative remark someone made to you ten years ago about a bad bridge has no bearing on what someone else may say to you today about your voice. People are not ganging up on you. Isolate their comments. Deal with them one at a time and then let them go. If you don't, your need for approval will escalate so greatly that you'll never get enough because the void it has to fill will have grown out of hand.

If you call someone twenty or forty times and don't receive a call back, don't personalize it. The reasons could be chaos at the office or the car is making that grinding-ticking-gurgling noise again and the BMW mechanic can't isolate or fix it. It could be trouble at home. Publishers and A&R executives are people too. They have kids and spouses and neighbors with obnoxious Dobermans just like normal folks.

People in the music business play "musical chairs" so much that you never know whether the guy you talked to yesterday will be there tomorrow. And much of our business is done in L.A., so you have to realize that when someone doesn't call back it could be due to his numerologist warning him not to speak with Scorpions while Mercury is in retrograde. Keep calling. Ask the receptionists you speak to what the climate is like in their respective offices, so if someone doesn't return your call, at least you know why. It usually has nothing to do with you.

I can't tell you how many times I've spent forty-nine dollars to express mail a tape to Fiji or France and then have waited six months for a response. But that slow response has nothing to do with my value as a songwriter or my work. Successful people are always busy. Right now, if they aren't busy with you, they're preoccupied with other priorities. One day, that priority will be you. Until then, force yourself to try to see their side of it.

While dedication is imperative if you want to be successful, it's important to have ways of distracting yourself from the inevitable rejection, so you don't get swallowed up in helplessness. Always have an alternative plan, another guy to see, six more people to call. Have hobbies. Give yourself a night with Playgirl's Mr. May or one of those women you see in the ads for 976-numbers. Lose yourself in something other than the bad meeting or the form letter you got back with your unopened tape. Play tennis, racquetball, jog, or do something else physical which you *can* control. It's contagious. The power you feel from physical exercise will spill over into your business dealings, too.

While I know music is your life, you still need friends, family, and an unconditional support group of civilians—nonmusic business people who will love you even when you're not winning. The nurturing of these people makes all the difference in the world. Try to balance your life so you attract and appreciate these kinds of pampering relationships. You have to wage war every day out there on the street, so you need a haven, a place to go, a friend to turn to—for your victories as well as for your failures.

It took me a long time to get it down, but what works best is rejecting rejection. There's a lot of talking to mirrors going on in my house. Pep talks before meetings and hard phone calls might seem a little over the edge for you, but they work for me. I often call my answering machine before a meeting and tell myself I can do it and never mind what the next guy says. Then no matter how the meeting goes, I get home to a friendly, uplifting message and it sounds like a dear friend comforting and supporting me.

After a bad interchange, don't look to someone else to pamper you. Be good to yourself first. I always buy myself flowers. Lately, I've been buying them before my meetings, so I come home to a pretty gift, no matter what the outcome. I used to hope my boyfriend would bring me flowers, but that meant it was his responsibility to tell me I was good. And it isn't. It's my responsibility. It's yours, too, for you.

Be armed for your meetings and phone calls. Don't approach them needy and vulnerable. Fortify yourself—in power clothes and power attitudes. Take charge of your meetings. Interview the person with whom you're talking or having the meeting. Don't let him put you on the defensive. Tell him what you want and what you can offer his company—not what you need from him or what you didn't get from everybody else. Never approach anybody out of weakness. Only from strength. Try saying something along the following lines, "Donald, I'm a hit songwriter. We can make a lot of money together. Listen to this." If he doesn't like or want your material, grant him that right and take your work somewhere else. Have lots of appointments lined up so a single "no" doesn't create a crisis.

It is imperative for you to separate yourself from what you write. You are not your song, even if every syllable absolutely happened to you. After the writing is done, you become the seller of that song, not its creator. So when it's time to market your material, you have to switch into your sales persona. Pretend you didn't write the song at all but are merely representing the person who did. That'll take some of the sting out of the rejection. If a publisher doesn't like your work, ask him how he'd suggest it be rewritten. That makes his job easier. No matter what you think of publishers, they'd rather say "yes" than "no," so work on establishing a relationship with them instead of making them feel bad for turning you down. Make notes of all their comments—good or bad. Then, when you're less emotionally involved, you can look at the problem objectively and see if their suggestions can work.

As a song peddler, you're no different from a Girl Scout trying to sell her cookies or a door-to-door encyclopedia salesman or a Hyundai dealer in Cucamonga. Not everybody will want what you have to offer. But think of all the people you've turned away at your door, and yet millions of Girl Scout cookies are sold every year. Almost every middle-class American home has a set of encyclopedias. And who ever heard of a Hyundai until a couple of years ago? You have to target your market and dig in. Don't let anybody's "no" be the last word. I've always tried to tell myself that each negative response is just one more I don't have to deal with again, and it gets me that much closer to the next "yes."

I've gotten a lot of courage from the rejection horror stories of my favorite songwriters. I hope you will learn from the following anecdotes, as I have, that you must keep on going, no matter what.

In the early stages of writer/producer Marti Sharron's career, if a publisher told her that her song wasn't right, she'd believe him, label the song "bad," and feel like she'd been run over by a bus. But later, as she gained some confidence, she learned to fight for what she wrote.

One A&R person rejected "Music Is the Way I Live" just because it didn't have the word "Dance" in the title. But Marti knew it was a strong song and kept on pushing. Good thing she did. A big hit for Patti LaBelle, the song went to number ten. If Marti hadn't felt strongly about the value of her tune, in spite of the A&R person's comment, it might still be in a dusty drawer somewhere.

But Marti wasn't always so sure of herself. At one point, just before she wrote "Jump (For My Love)," she was having such a bad time getting nowhere with her career, that she actually quit the business and went to work for a body shop, hustling customers via telephone to get their cars repaired. She relinquished her dreams of success as a songwriter/producer, realizing there is just so long you can hold out financially waiting for the big break that never comes.

Marti honestly asked herself if she could spend the rest of her life broke. She also needed to know what else she could do with her life, and what other possibilities would make her happy. She wondered long and hard if she would have to kill the artist in her heart in order to stick with a nine-to-five job. She had reached a terrible crossroads.

She worked at the body shop for a full year and never picked up a pencil. There was no demand on her to write, and every day that she pulled into the body shop, she told herself if she was supposed to be in the music business, something would happen to open the door for her.

And it did.

ASCAP assembled a panel of producers and publishers and invited some up-and-coming writers to have their work critiqued. Marti didn't think she should go, but her husband urged her to attend. As Marti sat through the critiques, hearing how the other writers' songs were being ripped apart, she wanted to bolt, but her husband was there with her, and for her, and wanted her to stay.

It's a good thing she did. Because soon after her critique, Linda Perry, a publisher at the meeting, signed her as a writer/producer. So Marti's way of coping with rejection was to walk away from from the business for a while, release all the demands on her writing, and let whatever was supposed to happen, happen. Perhaps if you've been heaping too much pressure on yourself, you should consider giving yourself your own break, and take some time to decompress.

Songwriters aren't the only ones who are rejected. Perry, who is now vice president of publishing at Lorimar, told me her worst rejection heartbreak occurred when she gave a producer an exclusive hold—or "freeze"—on one of her songs, then the song got cut, and never made it to the album. She learned her lesson—now she doesn't give freezes.

If a song Perry believes in doesn't get recorded by one artist, she goes after another producer and another artist, and gets it cut elsewhere. Some of the songs she publishes have taken five or six years to get recorded. So she's really had to believe in them.

Linda and Marti went to the Grammys together when Marti's song "Jump" was nominated. Linda noticed that Marti was greeting almost everybody there by name. "How do you *know* all these people," Linda wondered. "They all turned me down," Marti replied.

Songwriter/producer Jeff Barry, on the other hand, doesn't ever remember being rejected. Jeff didn't say he was *never* rejected—he said he didn't *remember*. I interpret this to mean that Jeff didn't dwell on the "no's." He simply plowed ahead on other songs and projects. He's the first to admit that he by-passed a lot of potential rejection because he wrote and produced his songs as masters. And eventually he even had his own label, so who was going to reject him? The moral to Barry's story is that he doesn't remember the rejection, which means he didn't miss a beat worrying about it. He just kept creating.

Lyricist John Bettis has had to deal with rejection all his life. He was a fat kid and the girls didn't like him, so he wrote to compensate. He was a good writer, which helped a little to overcome that awful teenage outsider feeling. But John had no idea of the world-class "no's" he'd ram into down the road.

In 1966, John and two friends formed a group called Spectrum and tried for two years to get a label deal. A&R people didn't just slam doors in this group's face, they slammed doors and *laughed* at them. Every record company in town turned them down. And so, two years later, the group broke up.

But then two of the members of the trio formed a duet, and got a deal. They called themselves the Carpenters.

With all his success as Richard Carpenter's co-writer, none of John's other songs got cut, even when the Carpenter's were the hottest. He wrote forty to fifty songs a year, every year, and nobody but the Carpenters recorded them.

It was terribly frustrating. But John knew it was impossible for one song a year to be so good and for the others to be so bad—so he kept on writing.

I'm glad he did. Otherwise, he wouldn't have written "Slow Hand," recorded by the Pointer Sisters, and one of his biggest copyrights to date.

Thomas Dolby says that his arrogance keeps him afloat when he's rejected. He'd written a big hit in England at the beginning of his career called "New Toy," for an artist named Lene Lovich. On the strength of that song, he went after a deal for himself as a singer/songwriter. Since everybody knew "New Toy," several companies were interested and A&M seemed the most enthusiastic. So Dolby's lawyer told all the other labels they were negotiating seriously with A&M and thanked them for their interest.

Meanwhile, at the eleventh hour, A&M changed its mind, the deal died, and the other labels weren't interested anymore. Dolby remembers it felt like a slap in the face. And yet, he didn't personalize it. Part of him knew it was only political. But another part of him was terrified that nobody would ever be interested in him as an artist again.

Devastated and in debt for several thousand pounds, which was a lot of money to him in those days, Thomas sublet his flat and fled from London to avoid the debts he'd run up with his lawyer, his landlord, the water company, the electric company, and the phone company.

Feeling temporarily safe in Paris, Thomas sang as a street musician and played in the subways for six months. Then he called the friend who sublet his London flat to find that the group Foreigner wanted him to come to New York to play keyboards for their *Foreigner Four* album. When that gig stretched from three days into a month, and Thomas had saved $7000, he paid off all his debts and returned to London, deciding to try the publishing companies this time, instead of the record companies.

It worked. He got a deal with EMI, which gave him carte blanche. His first album was no great shakes commercially. So Dolby went back into the studio to record some more tunes. One of them was "She Blinded Me with Science," which was added to the album released here on Capitol, and the single went to number five on *Billboard's* charts. It stayed there for six weeks. The album went to twelve, and was gold worldwide.

"I've been very lucky," Dolby admits. "I've had 100 percent permission to do what I wanted to do. The music business is easy if you have a lot of talent, along with the arrogance to not let anybody say no to you."

Randy Goodrum has been turned down like everybody else, but he doesn't dwell on it. He is very goal-directed. "It's a software program I was born with. If something doesn't work heading down one road, I'll try another route."

Randy is very determined. "All my songs are an effort to place. But I never take no as the final word." Even now his songs take an average of two years to get cut. "I'll Be over You" was turned down flat by Julio Iglesias but was a big hit for Toto.

"If I believe a song is a hit, nothing phases me. I keep plugging it. We all see the same people over and over again in this business. Sometimes they agree with me that my songs are hits and sometimes they don't. They can't always like everything I do."

But Randy wasn't so sure of himself at the beginning of his career. It took four years and ninety-five "no's" in Nashville alone, before his publisher finally placed "You Needed Me." Chris Christian declined the song for B.J. Thomas, and Chet Atkins also said no for Perry Como. But four years later, Anne Murray cut the song, won a Grammy, and it went all the way to number one.

"Dave Grusin told me something I've never forgotten," Randy recalls. "'All songs have a season.' When I've heard too many "no's" in a row, that keeps me on track."

Billy Steinberg started writing songs in 1968 when he was eighteen. He didn't have one cut until he was thirty, so there were twelve long years of rejection in between. "It motivated me," he says. "It made me angry. I'd grit my teeth and think about revenge. I was gonna show everybody they were wrong."

During those twelve years, unbeknownst to Billy, a relative of his sent a tape of Billy's songs to Jann Wenner, who publishes *Rolling Stone* magazine, in the hope that Jann would give the Steinberg family a professional opinion of Billy's talent, to see if he had what it took. After listening to Billy's tape, Jann said "no."

That just made Billy even more determined, even though he'd quit college and had gone to work in the family grape business.

When he and Tom Kelly wrote "Like a Virgin," the first half-dozen people they played it for thought it was completely off-the-wall. "The main comment was no one would ever sing a song with that lyric. Especially that title." But Billy and Tom believed in what they'd written. Later, it went to number one and stayed there for six weeks.

When "True Colors" was finished, a lot of people turned that one down, too. Billy's memory is a little fuzzy on the "no's," but he thinks he sent it to Don Grierson who sent it to Anne Murray, who passed. Cyndi Lauper, however, cut an imaginative version that was number one for two weeks. And later, the song was used in a Kodak commercial.

Publisher Alan Melina, of Famous Music, considers song plugging to be a competitive sport. He doesn't personalize rejection, because he didn't write the songs. If he doesn't place a song in a meeting, he knows the rejection is part of his job. The statistics are on his side.

When he came to Famous Music, there was a song in the catalog scheduled to return to its writers because it hadn't been cut and the two-year reversion clause was a month away from going into effect. The song was called "Nobody Loves Me Like You Do." Alan called the writers, told them he loved the song, and asked them for an extension. He got it. One hundred pitches and a year later, the tune still wasn't cut. He sent it to Arista three times, and each time, they passed. The fourth time, they kept it for Dionne Warwick. There were six songs held for her album, although they only needed four. And "Nobody Loves Me Like You Do" was one of the two that were dropped.

Then a colleague at Famous sent the song to Anne Murray's producer. That same week, Alan got a call from Arista saying they wanted the song to be a duet for Jermaine Jackson and a new female artist they were developing. Once again Alan got his hopes up.

The Anne Murray duet with Dave Loggins was a number one country record, but the song never made it to Jermaine's album. And Alan was upset. But it did make the first solo album of the girl singer on Jermaine's duet. Her name is Whitney

Houston. That album sold over thirteen million copies. All told, it took three years of relentless work to place the song. I'd say it was worth it, wouldn't you?

The bottom line is persistence. Alan says his success as a publisher comes from his faith that he's right. He doesn't personalize rejection or take it as a judgment of his taste. The criticism is out of his control.

Composer Martin Page says that at every level of his career there are new obstacles. "No matter how successful you are," he reminded me, "the rejection never stops."

Martin has some delicious rejection stories. When he wrote "These Dreams" with Bernie Taupin, they sent the song to several artists, including Paul Young and Bonnie Tyler, but didn't hear a word for six months. Then they played it for Kim Carnes, "who jumped on it." They even got together with her arranger, at her house, but later she called and said she wasn't going to cut the song. A month after that, Heart cut it. Nancy Wilson, their lead singer, sang it with a cold, and she sounded just like Kim. And her record was number one.

Page and Taupin also wrote "We Built This City," which was cut quickly by the Motels, and subsequently scrapped. Martin and Bernie pitched the song diligently for six months, but nobody wanted it. Then, one day, producer Peter Wolf asked Page if he had any songs for Jefferson Starship, but Martin frankly didn't think he did. The Starship was an old rock band, after all, and Martin didn't honestly think his songs would work for them. But Peter had heard "We Built This City," and he and his partner, Dennis Lambert, rewrote the chorus, saying they'd cut the song if the original writers gave them twenty percent. Martin and Bernie knew nobody else wanted it, and figured giving up twenty percent was no big loss. They were right. Because the Starship record went to number one.

But Page's best rejection anecdote is about the time Bernie Taupin wrote the lyric for a song titled "These Dreams." Stevie Nicks was supposed to write music to it, but she never did. The song Bernie eventually wrote with Martin became number one all over the world. I bet that took care of any bad feelings Bernie might of had from Stevie Nicks' rejection, wouldn't you think?

"When someone says 'no' to me, it makes me want to get a 'yes' on the next try," Page admits. "It inspires me to do better. I want everyone to like me and what I do. It makes me fight harder."

The sting of rejection stays with him for a long time, however. He remembers that early in his career, "the minute a publisher said 'no,' I got a hot flash of doom. It was all I could do to get out of his office before falling apart. It was like a girl saying 'I don't want to go out with you anymore' and totally demolishing me."

Now when he's rejected, Page always tries to force himself to see the positive side of it. Between being kicked in the stomach and the next move, he moans a lot to his manager. He calls everyone he loves and lets his feelings out, "can you believe this? That they would actually *do* this? We were *that* close! They don't know what they're doing!"

"I hate rejection," Page offers. "So I build a security system around myself. Then I always have a plan B. It isn't in my best interest to be morose. I have a philosophy: you win some, you lose some others. You can't have everything.

"But I don't like to dwell on the loss, because you are what you think you are. Any director who makes a lot of movies is bound to have a bomb some time. Even Spielberg. He made *1944*. Actually, failure now and then makes your music more emotional."

Narada Michael Walden is best known as a Grammy-winning producer. But he desperately wants to be an artist, too. In 1974, he was in a jazz fusion group called The Mahavishnu Orchestra, which released an album called "Apocalypse." Then he did a solo album called "Garden of Love Light" for Atlantic. Both did reasonably well on the jazz charts, but nowhere else. With his "I Cry, I Smile" album, also on Atlantic, he really wanted to tap the pop market, but nothing happened. At that point, Altantic records told Walden he either had to have a hit on his next album, or they'd drop him.

And that really made him reconsider what he was after. In 1978, disco was hot. So Walden cut "I Don't Want Nobody Else to Dance with You," which became a big dance hit.

But even so, when he was signed to produce some cuts on the second Whitney Houston album, Clive Davis rejected Walden's own songs. And that really hurt. "But you take 'no'and make it a strength for you," Walden philosophizes. He admits that while he didn't get any of his own songs on the second album, he did win a Grammy as producer.

"If you take a 'no' as 'no,' you become crusty. It's important to keep your heart fresh and young and optimistic. If you let people turn you down and keep you down, you begin to die."

Chrysalis publisher Tom Sturgess told me, "I'll play a song for every producer, A&R guy, film person, hairdresser, sister—anybody who'll listen." Tom has simplified the arithmetic of rejection, "Of 100 songs, ninety-two get rejected. Of those, three out of five get recorded. One out of three becomes a single."

Epic's A&R mogul/mensch Don Grierson maintains it's not all yesses on the other side of his desk, either, "Sometimes you're excited about a band and the other labels are too, and there's competition to sign that group. Even though you and the group have a terrific relationship, for some reason, they go to another label."

He has to deal with "no's" when he wants a certain producer for an act, and the producer passes. Don knows the producers and realizes they have previous commitments and conflicting schedules. He doesn't personalize a negative response.

Don was sure to remind me that even though a label may turn down an act, that label can change its mind. Michael Kaplan, at Epic, was following a band called Living Color around New York. "There was a bit of a buzz about them," Kaplan affirms, "and I went to see them. I liked the band. They didn't have hit material, but they were developing, and a couple of years later they had grown to the point where we signed them."

As for the ones that got away? "I've got too much to do to spend time being depressed. You evaluate why you didn't get the band, and correct the situation in the next negotiation."

Sounds like good advice to aspiring songwriters as well.

In 1975, Christopher Cross sent a tape to Warner Brothers, who sent the following reply: "Your music shows promise, but we find the lyric banal and full of platitudes. We like your voice, but the production is string-drenched. Keep in touch."

Christopher naively believed they were idiots, "I couldn't understand how these people could be so stupid to not see my genius. I thought the music was incredibly special and well-formed and ready for the radio. I figured I'd stumbled upon the wrong person, who wasn't a visionary. I had a typically confident and delusionary attitude. Instead of keying in on their comments, I was too defensive and ignored them.

"Two years later, I listened to that tape again and started to realize Warner Bros. was right. The arp was up too high, my lyrics were trite, so I concentrated on correcting the things they criticized."

In 1977, Cross made another tape and sent it to Warner Bros. again. They remembered him. They still liked his voice and were much more encouraging. Unfortunately, they still didn't hear a hit single, though they did say he was missing by just a little.

In 1978, Cross made another tape, which contained "Ride Like the Wind," "Sailin,'" and "The Light Is On." This time, Warner Bros. said: "We still like your voice. We think you're a great musician, but we still don't hear a hit." So he sent them another tape with "Say You'll Be Mine" on it. That was the one they were looking for.

In between his contacts with Warner Bros., Christopher sent his tape elsewhere. Arista turned him down flat. Roger Birnbaum at A&M wanted Kip Cohen to sign Christopher. But they passed because they'd just signed The Captain and Tennille. One small record company was mildly interested, wanting to do a singles deal. But nobody wanted to do an album. I wonder how they all felt when Christopher had seven top 10 singles in a row and his first album was on the charts for 400 weeks.

Jimmy Webb was very frank with me, "The first thing you're going to have to know if you're going to do this for a living is that there's going to be an eighty percent or better rejection rate. If you're talking about top 10 success, then it's even higher."

The saga of Webb's early days is fascinating. As he recalls, "None of the record companies were interested in me at all. I hit 'em all. All the big ones—RCA, Capitol, you name it. I was going in with my songs and left tapes. I was eighteen and was also going to school at San Bernardino Valley College. I was commuting from San Bernardino. There was a big financial problem because my parents had moved back to Oklahoma and things were pretty scruffy.

"I didn't have any furniture or a piano up here to play and slept on a mattress in an apartment where some school friends lived. I'm sure the way the story should've ended is that I should have given up and gone back to Oklahoma to become a farmer. I was pretty discouraged.

"To get by, I did lead sheets because I picked the skill up from a guy named Bob Ross who was a great music copyist in this town. I got paid five bucks each. Bob was a great chum of mine, in fact his company, Hambone Music, still owns Jimmy Webb copyrights because they were trading me studio time for publishing.

"The first pure Jimmy Webb song that I ever got a record on was 'My Christmas Tree,' which they put on the Supreme's Christmas album." Motown was also looking for a follow-up single for an artist named Paul Peterson who'd had a hit with a bubble gum song called "She Can't Find Her Keys." Jimmy tried hard to write them one. Anxiously, he brought in a song he liked a lot, but which had an unusual structure—AAA. Motown told Webb the song needed a chorus after each verse. So they passed. Incidentally, the song they rejected was "By the Time I Get to Phoenix."

Even after having two songs nominated in the same year for Song of the Year at the Grammys, people were still saying no to Jimmy Webb. Bones Howe asked him to write something unique for a vocal group called the Association, and Jimmy did. But they passed . . . on a song called "MacArthur Park."

The rejection didn't stop there. Webb remembers producing Cher, "She was on the cover of every magazine, had just broken up with Sonny, and had her own TV show. But our album bombed. You should always beware when you get that little tickle inside that tells you that you've got it made. I used to be a pilot. Whenever a pilot thinks he's got it made, he's in trouble. Just as you're peaking, that can sometimes be a very dangerous time." Webb gave a warning, "Anybody who sets himself up to thinking that he's always going to be on top is going to be in emotional trouble."

And plans and ideas don't always pan out, even for veterans like Webb. "I have a song on an Amy Grant album called 'If These Walls Could Speak,'" he said recently. "When I wrote it, I heard Waylon Jennings' voice singing it. I keep sending it to him, but so far, it hasn't fitted in with his plans. I wrote a song for Sinatra called 'Winter Clothes.' He passed. And I wrote a song for Dionne Warwick called 'Acting Alone.' Passed again. Everybody turns me down—Diana Ross, Julio Iglesias—everybody. So you have to swallow hard and keep going."

I have quotes from these pages on yellow post-its and they're stuck all over my fridge, my mirrors, my dashboard, and my office, because when I'm flattened by rejection, which happens at least three times a week, I'm inspired and comforted by my colleagues' struggles and victories. So I suggest you mark this chapter and come back to it as needed.

CHAPTER TWELVE

Little Victories Count Too

I know you have big dreams and expectations for yourself. Nobody gets anywhere in our business without them. But you must acknowledge small successes too. While they may seem insignificant compared to a gold record or a number one chart song, a little victory can make a tremendous difference in a writer's life.

For example, I love being funny. It doesn't make me a better writer or consultant, but I sure do love to tell a joke and hear people laugh. I collect good jokes—not just for the ego boost—for the short-run payoffs. When I tell a joke, I know within seconds if the tellee liked it. If he does, it makes me feel good immediately. It's healthy, it's good for my morale and it gives me confidence to try other things that are harder for me.

In our business the payoffs can be enormous, but they're usually a long way off. It occurred to me one day that instead of dwelling on who rejected me and how hard they did so, I felt better if I could be funny. I nursed my comic talents along until I now feel very competent and confident about my sense of humor. I find that I can usually count on it in a pinch to get me out of trouble.

Most of you are, and should be, obsessed with one thing: having hits. You spend all your days and nights writing, rewriting, and fighting for air time. Songs, songs, songs. But even if you play a song for a publisher today who absolutely loves it, and is desperate to make a deal with you, it could still be five years—or never—before a record is released and you actually see some tangible recognition for your efforts.

Now suppose Harry Hitmaker loves your song, gives you a fat advance, and swears it's Whitney Houston's next single. You're hyped to the hilt, feeling you're a genius, believing you've finally made it. Every split second of your life is devoted to that song making you famous, rich, and somebody. You become addicted to the payoffs of that tune, unable to function or move, waiting for it to validate you.

Friends may caution you not to put such a great demand on one song, but then Whitney *does* cut it. Harry says you might get the single. Then you *do* get the single. It'll be shipped in ten days. Then six. Two. Eighteen hours. Then the release date is mysteriously put back until after the Fourth of July. Then the label's PR chief quits to farm jicama in Oregon. Or the company is greenmailed by a pablum/munitions conglomerate that will only release songs with "herb" in the title. The entire album is scrapped and you're hung out to dry.

Not only are you disappointed that you didn't get the success everyone promised you, the validation you've been waiting for all your hungry life, but caught up in all the hype, you've forgotten to do your *job*, which is to write. And now you're sputtering on empty and can't function.

That's why you have to keep track of your little victories and validate them—especially those that have nothing to do with writing. We're so focused and single-minded, we often forget that this is real life, where a great deal more than gold records matter. There are plenty of things we do in the course of a day that are important—even if they aren't validated by the industry.

I never was good at anything except writing. I never tried to be. All I ever wanted was to be a writer. Why should I have bothered with hobbies, I thought. Were they kidding? I was a songwriter. I had no designs on being the best anything else. All I wanted to do was write. And that's all I did. My life was obsessive and hollow.

Sure, my songs were getting cut and I had hits on the radio, but on the days when nobody was taking my calls, for whatever reason, I always felt like a wad of dirty chewing gum someone was trying to scrape off the sole of his Gucci shoe. It didn't seem fair that I'd do so well on one level and feel so inconsequential on another. So I had to figure out how *not* to feel badly.

I was urged to find a hobby. But I was only interested in music. Of the 211 courses offered at UCLA extension, the only one I wanted to take was the Songwriter's Workshop, and I'd already taken that. In fact, I was teaching it.

Then someone tactfully suggested that I learn to cook. He said eating take-out food while standing up in front of my open fridge had its merits, but it wasn't the only way to go. What, I wondered, did Santa Monica need with another good cook with eighty kinds of imported, yuppie mustard?

However, after bachelor number thirty-two walked out on dinner number three, I decided to take a cooking class. At first, it was embarrassing not being able to chop vegetables in that machete style like my other expert classmates. But I worked at it, took remedial garlic one Saturday, and caught up. I started to feel good about being accomplished in something new. I actually enjoyed going to class and looked forward to that evening away from music. I made new friends in that class who didn't judge me by whether I still had my *Billboard* bullet. These were the first unconditional relationships I'd had since college. And it sure felt great.

Being good at something other than music makes me feel more balanced and accomplished. On days when nobody calls me back, I cook. It's creative, because I decorate my baking with flowers from my garden and make them beautiful. It prevents burn-out. And it's satisfying because my cake testers give me feed back immediately. "Hey, this is delicious" has become as rewarding a response as "Hey, this song is a hit."

I know how focused you are and how single-minded you need to be to make it. But you must have things you're good at that are completely and totally satisfying in the short run. This lends you momentum to keep on working on your own songwriting. So if you don't have hobbies, you should find some.

Here's what some of my clients do.

One man, who was putting his fist through bricks because of how slowly his music life was moving, had a garage sale and sold absolutely every item, even the twenty-five cent pocket books. Even though the sale took place during a monsoon, my client discovered himself to be very assertive and refused to let any customers out of his apartment without buying something. He controlled the situation, something we can't always do as writers. He experienced power from the success of that venture, as well as a major sense of accomplishment. He planned a garage sale, he gave a garage sale, and sold everything. That was a *big* little win. It gave him some badly needed momentum, self-esteem, and courage to keep working on his music.

Another client was complaining about how unrewarded she felt about her songs. Then she discovered gardening. Now she plants a carrot and gets a carrot. In our business, you can plant a potato and get a subpoena, so it's very gratifying to plant a seed and watch it grow.

Now that she has little victories every time something new pops out of the earth, she has much less pressure on her to make her writing pay off for her immediately, so she feels she's getting somewhere with something. And she's writing better than ever.

At the end of each day, I make a list of all the "wins" I experience during the day. Not just the obvious stuff, like gold records, book deals, and fat checks, but the little things, too. Here's a partial list from yesterday:

♦ Took my walk as planned, even though I would've preferred to stay in bed and watch Wimbledon.

♦ Remembered to take my vitamins.

♦ Bought travel insurance.

♦ Didn't throw anything breakable at the TV when Arantxa Sanchez lost to Steffi Graf.

♦ Meditated.

♦ Did my back exercises.

♦ Did my thigh exercises.

♦ Finally picked up my yellow pants at the cleaners.

♦ Ate dinner sitting down.

♦ Had three terrific sessions with clients.

Try listing your own little victories at the end of each day. I know you'll start to feel "fuller" and less needy about your songs when you can consistently acknowledge you're winning in one activity, even seemingly insignificant ones. This, in turn, will help your writing, because you'll be approaching it from strength, not need.

CHAPTER THIRTEEN

What to Do If Your Father Thinks You're a Bum

Let's assume you've done your mental homework and have developed a little routine to overcome rejection, and it's working. Let's also assume you've gotten into the good habit of making "little victory" lists every day, and your confidence as a songwriter is in pretty good shape. Maybe it's taken you several weeks of dedication to reach this plateau, and you're proud of yourself. You should be.

But then along comes some member of your family who wipes you out completely with a brief, snotty remark about the "goddamn noise" you're producing or the medical school your *successful* sibling just graduated from. And you're back to feeling rotten about yourself and your chances for success.

I know this dynamic well. I'm a rock-and-roll refugee myself. My father threw me out of his house one January morning when it was fifty-five below zero because he couldn't stand me strumming my guitar one more minute, and I couldn't bear to stop. So when my clients tell me they have unsupportive parents, I know what they're talking about.

One of the few parents I've ever encountered who rooted for his child to succeed as a songwriter was the enthusiastic New York cabbie in the movie *Fame* who proudly broadcasted his son's songs from his dented, yellow hack. A majority of the other parents I've met think writing songs is a notch lower than being a drug pusher or mass murderer.

So it's not just *your* mother who doesn't understand. No mother does. I've never spoken to Mrs. Webb, Mrs. Dylan, or Mrs. Springsteen personally, but I'll bet you a Hewlett-Packard Laserjet II printer that they'd have been a lot happier if their offspring went into another profession. Anything that had better medical coverage and less night work.

One of our greatest occupational hazards as writers is needing the approval of people who won't give it. No matter how successful we become, and no matter how lofty the praise from other sources, we still ache for that long distance call from the kitchen in Kentucky saying "we're proud of you."

Leikin's Fifth Law: Don't wait for your parents' approval—give it to yourself. Parental approval usually doesn't come until we've already made it. In the meantime, even if you've signed on to be a songwriter, don't expect your parents to throw you a party when you get your union card.

Why can't a mother can't be happy that her child is gifted and wants to be an artist? Beats me. I frankly think we, as songwriters, should form some sort of support group for ourselves to combat the lack of parental enthusiasm for our life's work. We could call it Songwriters Against Parents: SAP. We could sell T-shirts, pens, coffee mugs and satin jackets. Our parents, on the other hand, could form their own support group: Parents of Struggling Songwriters and Entertainers—POSSE.

Far be it from me to ever take the side of a parent, but twenty years have passed since that January morning I was evicted, and with time, I've come to claim a certain enlightenment on the subject. Non-creative parents don't *understand* what we do and because they don't understand, they are frightened. In order to continue in their role as parents, they feel they must steer us away from what they don't understand, onto a path that is more familiar.

Unfortunately, they *do* understand groaning awake in the morning and stuffing themselves into uncomfortable suits to take their places on clogged, smoggy freeways that lead them to jobs they abhor, but which *provide stability.* Whoopie. And anything that deviates from this norm is threatening to many a parent's security system. So they do their best to sabotage their children's creative dreams.

The one client I feel is the closest to smashdom of any undiscovered songwriter I've ever met called the morning after Father's Day in terrible shape. I became enraged when I heard what his father-in-law had said about him at a family party the night before. Attended by blue-collar, hard-working people, one of the guests asked my client—let's call him Chip—what he did for a living. Before Chip had a chance to answer, his father-in-law opened his mouth and jumped in, "He does nothing." My client was wiped out.

It seems his father-in-law is a carpenter. He got Chip into that union and before Chip quit to write fulltime, he made a very comfortable living in that trade. His father-in-law is angry that Chip quit a secure job to speculate in the music business. To add insult to injury Chip is now doing something the older man doesn't understand. Moreover, the father-in-law doesn't have any influence in the music business and is helpless to push Chip along. So you see we're dealing with an escalating and volatile situation.

If you're a carpenter, you take a load of lumber at the beginning of the day, get out your hammer and nails, and you whack away. At the end of the day, you've built yourself (or a paying customer) a garage. Wood + work = garage. The formula is simple.

But if you write songs, you could spend the whole day sitting at your piano without producing a single melody line or phrase worth keeping. Nobody can *see* that. Nobody can hear that, either. There is no short-term pay off. Nothing in a developing songwriter's life is tangible. You certainly can't show a civilian parent a page of crossed-out scribbles and boast "hey—look what I did today, Pa." You know that even though you don't see the lines and phrases you want on your page, they are somewhere in your subconscious, waiting to pop out at any moment. So while you don't see your "garage" at the end of your work day as a songwriter, the garage *is* in there. So are all the materials for it. The final product just comes out later, perhaps only one nail at a time. But that doesn't mean it isn't a garage.

Don't try to convince your family that you work as hard as any lawyer or doctor. Instead, I'd suggest you make peace with yourself and your goals. Know that you're *going* to be successful, in spite of your lack of parental support, and just move ahead with your work. And your work is writing—not chasing after approval for your decision to write.

Chip is not my only client with parental problems. Sandy, another superbly gifted writer, has a family that makes George and Martha from *Who's Afraid of Virginia Woolf* look like the Cosby's. Sandy grew up a very sensitive child in an angry house of unfulfilled people, all doing things they *had* to do but didn't want to. These people were stuck—and mean. So when Sandy announced she was going to be a songwriter instead of an English teacher, it really hit the fan and she left home. For fifteen years Sandy heard nothing but glowing reports about her successful brother—the lawyer with the private airplane—and her *younger* sister who married a cardiologist/community leader and had three children by natural childbirth.

But when Sandy went home last year for a funeral, she found out that her lawyer-brother had been recently disbarred for embezzlement, and the married sister didn't have the courage to leave her philandering husband, and now weighs in at 300 pounds. Yet in spite of the staggering failures of her siblings, Sandy is still considered the black sheep of the family, because she's a songwriter.

Even when I was a staffwriter and had already chalked up a couple of hits, whenever I fell into a career slump, my mother felt compelled to remind me of the college education I had, that she *didn't* have, and about the graduate work I did at the Sorbonne, which qualified me to be a translator, perhaps at the U.N. She'd segue into how I could still write—it would make a wonderful hobby for a girl. Maybe I could send some poems in to the *Ladies Home Journal*. Or *Redbook*. But she could see absolutely no reason to struggle in a business of "whipped cream" when "pot roast and boiled potatoes were right at my finger tips."

I will tell you that *after* I started having hits, both my parents recruited all the little old ladies on their retired Florida beach to call the local radio stations daily to request my songs. The tunes somehow became *their* songs, and the bunch of them were furious with me for not giving them my gold and platinum records to hang over the fireplace.

Parents aren't the only ones with whom songwriters must struggle to keep their self-esteem. A writer must also deal with the strangers who ask what he or she does do for a living. When you say you're a songwriter, they invariably ask what you've written. They don't ask doctors to name their patients, or lawyers to list their cases, but they always ask writers for their credits. If you're asked to give yours and have to say "nothing you'd know yet," they respond with a disparaging "oh . . . ." You're left feeling like you have unpleasant body odor.

On days when I'm feeling insecure and don't want to risk being emotionally flattened, I say I'm a gynecologist and quickly ask what the *other* person does. It doesn't matter if the questioner is a bag lady or a chairman of the board, I just keep barraging him or her with questions about his/her line of work to keep the subject permanently changed. I don't want to have to justify my job or my existence to a stranger whose indifference can hurt me.

Our parents, and people in general, *do* claim us once we're successful. But getting there is up to us. Be aware of this, accept it, and write to make yourself happy. Gain your own approval, not anybody else's. That's where hits come from, anyway.

CHAPTER FOURTEEN

Make Deadlines
Work for You

Not only must we often deal with disapproving relatives in our business but we often have to work with people who "need it yesterday." Some writers can't cope with this panic any better than with their parents' lack of support. They continue creating at their own slow pace and miss a lot of opportunities. But developing songwriters, especially those who don't sing, produce, or have their own label deal yet, need every break they can get. It would serve you well to be known as someone who can be called at the last minute to deliver a great, custom-tailored song—on time.

During our initial consulting sessions many of my clients confess to me that they've been working on songs for months and are horribly frustrated by not being able to finish them more quickly. The solution I suggest is one that works very well for me—I give myself a deadline.

Even if I know there isn't one, I create one, to give myself focus and a sense of purpose. That way I have a reason to get up in the morning, and more important, a reason to pick up my pen. Then, when there really is a deadline, I'm used to working under pressure and can perform my writing tasks creatively, confidently—business as usual.

That's what got me my first staff writing job at Almo. I'd worked steadily with a professional manager from Warner Brothers who moved over there. He always seemed to call me in the middle of the night in need of a song for somebody named Nunzio by the next day. And somehow, I always brought him one. He didn't always love what I wrote, but he usually did, and certainly applauded my effort. He was impressed that I could put my own persona aside and write a song that would be believable for the artist-of-the-week to sing. And while I resented the panic of the deadline, I secretly loved it.

When that publisher called me, I felt important. And needed. Even though I knew he called all his staffwriters to give them the same assignment, I wanted to be in there competing with the best of them.

Later, when I started writing movie themes, the deadlines got tougher. Sometimes I had as little as eight hours to write a theme for a movie that the producers had been working on for over a year. At first, I was hired because some better known writer didn't deliver on time. I wasn't a "star" yet, but I had earned a reputation for being reliable, so I got the gigs.

What's interesting is that when I had a month to write a film theme, I took the whole month to do it. When I only had one night, I still got it done and was just as happy with the results. There is something about having a deadline that creates the energy to meet it.

Early in my career, a very successful man told me that when you want something done, ask someone busy to do it. If a guy has to be surgically removed from his sofa where he has spent the day in his L.A. Ram jammies, it will certainly take him longer to get even the simplest things done than someone who is already in high gear.

Like athletes, writers have to keep in shape. If you only jog once a month, you'll ache for weeks afterwards. You'll resist jogging again and find a thousand excuses not to make the effort. But if you do it every day, you stay fit.

Energy creates energy. I don't know if Einstein would have put it quite that way, and I won't pretend for a minute to be a scientist, but I get the most done on days when I have the most to do. Some people hide under their quilts at the thought of having a crowded schedule ahead of them, but I love it. The secret is starting with something easy. I begin with my back exercises. That doesn't require creativity or innovation. It's all rote. And even though my eyes might not be open yet, I feel very accomplished when I've completed something before breakfast.

I know lots of very talented "writers" who are independently wealthy but never get anywhere with their careers. While everybody else is home in a hot panic writing, these "writers" are unfocused and just float. Instead of working on their songs and their careers, they make appointments for pedicures from people named Xilary and wait for their nutritionists to call back to tell them if it's okay to have a kumquat. The families of these writers set up trust funds for them so they get by nicely on the income. But they don't have the fight necessary to go out there and win. What's missing is the killer instinct that is absolutely mandatory in the music business. While I'm not suggesting the trust funders in the group sign it all over to the bag people, anybody who wants to be successful has to go after it or it'll never happen. No matter who you are, nobody in the music business is ever going to *give* you anything. Ever. Once, an ex-partner of mine bragged that his publisher gave him a butter-soft Italian leather sofa for Christmas. Later, to his horror, he discovered that the publisher deducted the cost from his royalties. So much for gifts.

Stress can be productive. Some writers discover that once they have a hit and have become financially secure, they get lazy. They find that when they wrote songs because they loved to write, they seemed to feel better about their work and themselves than when they were writing just for money and to maintain expensive lifestyles. For the eight years I was a staffwriter, as soon as the ink was dry on my contracts, I'd start to worry about whether or not my option would be picked up the following year. And because of that, I worked harder than ever and pushed myself to write better. The anxiety kept me pushing myself to write higher quality songs. So the stress paid off.

Having a deadline legitimizes your work. If a friend calls you while you're working on a song and invites you to lunch, the chances are good that your friend won't take "I'm writing" for an excuse and will probably keep on you until you say yes. But if you tell your pal you have a deadline, it's more likely that your commitment will be respected and you'll be left to your work.

Some film composers I know wait until the night before a scoring session to write their cues. I couldn't stand it, but it works for them. I guess they wouldn't keep getting hired if they didn't deliver. I prefer the luxury of time to rewrite, but that's my process. Figure out what works best for you and set your own deadlines accordingly.

As a consultant, I speak at songwriting associations all over the continent. Before I arrive, I give the members of a particular organization their assignment via their newsletter, usually a month before my seminar. Then I come to town and critique the songs written for my assignment. I initiated this practice after my first visit to the Arizona Songwriters Association in Phoenix. I discovered that the quality of their writing improved 2000 percent from my first seminar. The reason? I realized that be-cause of the specifics of my assignment, the writers had focus, guidelines, and time pressure. The combination of these three ingredients created an energy that had very positive results.

If you're a prolific writer, you may think you don't need to do assignment writing. But there are five reasons why I recom-mend you try:

1. In our competitive business, we all have days and even weeks when we've been writing in such isolation that we feel even if we put ads in the paper saying we have cash to give away to the first fifteen callers, our phones still wouldn't ring. So this deadline assignment will cre-ate a need for your songs that otherwise wouldn't exist and will make you feel you're at the hub of the business, instead of on the fringes.

2. Since the isolation of writing can often feel like a form of S&M, having an assignment helps create structure in an otherwise unstructured day.

3. Fulfilling your commitment to yourself gives you a sense of accomplishment in the short run when most of the payoffs in our business are very far away.

4. It proves to you that you can do it, so when you're asked to do something on short notice, you have the confidence from your last assignment to know you can do it again.

5. You get a new song. Even if the person you write it for doesn't cut it, somebody else probably will.

I think you'll find that although setting deadlines for yourself is stressful, achieving your goals is bound to give you courage, confidence, and momentum. And nobody ever has too much of that.

EXERCISE ONE

If you want to write "on assignment," but you aren't in contact with top artists yet, or you can't command the fees just now that justify your work, give yourself an assignment. Mark the due date in your appointment book, just as if it were a meeting with Clive Davis, president of Arista Records. If you normally write a song every two weeks, make your deadline for this one ten days away.

For this song, you might want to try writing one that's funny. Most of us write serious love songs all the time and that gets a little old. So write one just for the sport of it. One of my clients did this and came up with a great tune about fat thighs. This songwriter, who was always upset with himself for not getting his work done on time, enjoyed the experience and felt very accomplished for meeting his deadline. He also had fun working on it. And writing should always be fun.

In your appointment book, mark down that you worked on your song each day you *do* work on it. When you get it finished, check off that fact in your appointment book, too. Then reward yourself in some tangible way for your accomplishment. I have an account to which I transfer a specific amount of money every time I finish something I write on a deadline. If I think I did a particularly good job, I give myself a bonus, too. Even if you only give yourself a dollar, you'll still feel like you've received a reward for a job well done.

CHAPTER FIFTEEN

How to Cope with Writers' Three Biggest Emotional Problems

Songwriters have to deal with an endless stream of anxiety-provoking situations. The toughest ones are: not feeling like writing when you have to write; feeling "stabbed" by a painful occurrence in some other area of your life; and finishing something and feeling all at loose ends. Let's discuss them one at a time.

I DON'T FEEL LIKE WRITING TODAY

Let's suppose you have two precious hours to write, but you find to your dismay that you just don't *feel* like writing. The first thing you must *not* do is get on your own back for not making better use of the time you fought so hard to set aside. All writers frequently find themselves not in the mood to write, even the most prolific and successful ones. Even when they *have* to write.

I've decided to show you the internal process I went through the last time I didn't really feel like writing. Perhaps you'll recognize parts of yourself in my account and realize you're not alone. This is how it went:

I don't feel like writing today. I know I should, because I'm a writer and writers write. But I just don't feel like writing today. I don't have anything to say.

Aren't I the one who says that if you don't have something new to say, don't say anything? So how can I say one thing and do another? I guarantee you that somebody from Brooklyn, on the Donahue Show, will bust me if I get trite now. No point in ruining a good career with a bad song. By not writing today, I'm actually saving my reputation. Good thing I caught it in time. So I think I'll put my notebook away. There. I'll do the laundry instead.

But oh God, I feel guilty!

I'm *supposed* to be writing. I'm *supposed* to be romantic and clever, making people smile and dream in ways they never have before. A few years ago, the only thing I wanted was time to write whenever I felt like it. I cancelled everything I had planned today, gift-wrapped the eight hours and gave them to myself to write.

Now I don't *feel* like writing.

Because I honestly think I should be spending my life doing something more meaningful to the world than just being a little bit famous. Maybe my father was right. Maybe this is not a job for an adult. Shouldn't I consider the big picture, not just the small page? Shouldn't I be marching barefoot across America in the rain to protest nuclear war or something? Shouldn't I be saving the salmon or running for the Senate? I'd be great in the Senate. Senator Leikin. They'd probably misspell my name, but I could change it. Molly Kennedy has a ring to it. I could do a lot of good in the United States Senate. Lots more than I'm doing here, having to stay inside and write when I don't feel like it. And I'd be paid every two weeks like a real person.

Looking longingly out the window at some beautiful, bare-foot, blonde children running through the sprinklers, I know if I went for a walk—just for an hour—I'd see a thousand windy sailboats in the bay. Wouldn't some sun be good for me? I mean a person could die up here in this office for lack of vitamin D.

I still don't feel like writing. Because I wrote like a champion last week and I know I peaked. I couldn't possibly do better than that now. So shouldn't I quit while I'm ahead?

If you don't feel like writing, what *do* you feel?

Well, I feel like sneaking off to a San Francisco bed & break-fast with what's his name, or hearing every song I ever wrote played back to back on a Solid Gold weekend. I feel I'd like to spend the day shopping at Neiman Marcus, buying whatever I want and charging it to BMI. I feel that I want to look like Meg Ryan in *When Harry Met Sally*. I feel like seeing an eighteen-wheeler full of crisp, new hundred dollar bills pull into my driveway. I *don't* feel like writing.

Because what would I say? The quick brown fox jumped over the lazy dog? A big blue frog played Mozart for Mayor Koch? Do you like lemon-lime or butterscotch?

It was Friday night and both of us were lonely. . . . No, I already wrote that one.

Okay, okay. I'll confess. I don't feel like writing because I know all the good songs have already been written.

Attention all unclaimed song ideas in the universe: the lady in the khaki Naf Naf warm up suit is ready for a song. Naf Naf. Half 'n Half. Steffi Graf. Gee, I'd like her autograph. Notes appear upon the staff and look out, I am writing a song.

That's how one of my days went. Did you see some of yourself in that process? The last few lines I wrote were silly and whimsical, but they have rhythm and they rhyme and, best of all, they led me to a few words I wanted to keep and develop into a song. So by trusting myself to have it in me, I just went with it and eventually got rolling.

As writers, we all face days like the one I just described. The bad days don't go away when we have hits on the radio. I feel that being able to write and having the time to write are gifts we should treasure. I also feel that writing something every day helps keep you in shape to write. Some writers disagree with me, and I have to allow them their own work habits. But like everything else we do, we'll do better on some days than on others. On the bad ones, we have to develop the professionalism and objectivity to know when to go out and play a set of tennis and when to stay home at the piano and give it another twenty minutes.

If you don't want to write, or if you feel you have nothing to say, write about it—at least you're writing something. Once you get some words on paper, the page isn't blank anymore. It isn't your enemy anymore, either. Since songs are usually about feelings, if you write about what you're feeling—even if it has nothing do with with a song—you're still in process. You never know which word or idea is going to spark another and click you into high songwriting gear.

If you feel you don't want to write today, try three things. First, make a deal with yourself to try writing for half an hour, then you'll go do whatever you want. During your thirty minutes, write down what you're feeling, even if you're craving a Dove Bar or you can't decide which screening of *Steel Magnolias* you want to see. Get something on paper. You never know what's going to come out. Like me, I bet you'll be pleasantly surprised.

Next, try writing a song called "I Don't Want to Write To-day" in verse/chorus format. Make it uptempo, two and a half minutes long, and include in the lyric all the things you'd rather be doing.

Then, do something very nice for yourself for sticking with it and writing even when you didn't want to. Remind yourself— out loud—that you earned this reward for the good work you did. It's the child in a creative personality that does the writing, and if that child is constantly rewarded for his good work, he'll be much more willing to work for you next time you need him.

THE PLEASURES OF PAIN

I'm sure you've noticed that because you're sensitive, which you have to be in order to write, you're upset a lot of the time. As songwriters, the day we pay off our first guitar picks, they sign us up for the Pain of the Month Club.

However, because we're artists, when we're upset we can use the discomfort as grist for our creative mills. One of my clients, let's call him David, has chronic back problems and is incapacitated much of the time. Just when he thinks he's healed, another vertebra goes out. When he came to me, David's pain was so intense, it was keeping him from writing. I asked him what the pain looked like.

"A mean, black crab," he told me. "Grows another claw every time some part of my body doesn't hurt. His job is to make sure *everything* is excruciating." I told him to write that down, and save the image.

David didn't feel like writing a *song* about his monster, but he wrote a long letter, and in his prose there were some descriptive passages he can use in his work later on. By writing about what he was feeling, no matter what form it took, he was able to purge himself of his anger and helplessness. Pain is passive. Writing is active. So when you're writing, no matter what you're writing, you're in control and much more powerful than when you're simply a victim.

Another of my clients, let's call her Marcie, had been breaking up and making up and breaking up with the same man for ten years. They'd finally said goodbye nicely. But there were some days and nights when Marcie was completely blocked by this break-up, "I can't write 'cause the only words that come out of my pen are about Ed. I'm afraid to answer my phone 'cause I'm sure it's him. But I'm also terrified it isn't, and that nobody else will ever love me."

When I asked Marcie if she wrote this down, she snapped. "I *said* I'm not gonna write about him anymore." So I suggested she talk it into a tape recorder. I knew it hurt, but it was all original and would make a great song someday. I told Marcie that when she was happy again, she wouldn't remember what she'd said to me and it would be gone forever. As an antidote to her suffering, I suggested she buy herself flowers.

"I already did," she sobbed. "Daisies. I bought white ones. But they turned gray, and wilted from the sadness before I even got 'em home." I told Marcie if *she* didn't write that down *I* would. So she did. And you should hear the song it grew up to be.

Ethel and the Shameless Hussies, who record for MCA, have a song on a recent album that's called "I'm Taking My Pain to the Bank." Sometimes I feel if I did that with mine, they'd have to open a new branch just for me. "Molly's Savings and Loan." CD's wouldn't mean cash deposits in my bank—the letters would stand for consolidated devastation. Or certified dilemmas. Or constant duplicity.

So on those days and nights when you share my feelings and those of my clients and colleagues, put your hurt to work, just as the successful writers of our favorite songs have done and will continue to do.

Next time you're experiencing physical or emotional pain, try and write a letter to the source, letting all your anger out. Use as many four-letter words as you want. But be as visually descriptive as possible.

After you've diffused the anger, go back to your letter and circle the passages that are original, and pat yourself on the back for coming out of the experience with something valuable to add to your repertoire.

Now, write a verse/chorus song about what you're feeling.

And in the future, always keep a list of your most intense emotional experiences in a special section of your notebook, so you can easily refer back to them when you're writing and need something original.

COPING WITH COMPLETION ANXIETY

It's important for you to realize that the creative process has three identifiable stages: getting ready to create, creating, and letting go. The latter is a phase most of us don't recognize, but which is every bit as important as the first two.

You'd think you'd feel elated and triumphant after finishing a writing project, wouldn't you? Well, you do, temporarily. But then you crash. This terrible letdown, which I call "completion anxiety," is similar to the postpartum depression women experience after giving birth. All artists suffer from it. The smart ones recognize it, accept it as a normal part of their creative process, get through it, and move on.

When we're in the middle of a song, we're obsessed with what we're creating. And that only intensifies as draft after draft is written and rewritten, demos are made, mixed, remixed, and tapes are duplicated, labelled, and mailed. Then suddenly it's over. And there's nothing to do.

At this stage of songwriting, we don't control our work anymore. The U.S. post office does, along with unknown receptionists at publishing companies, and mystery A&R personnel. The emptiness, uncertainty, and creative impotence we feel as writers at this stage leave us completely hollow.

Often, a songwriter's first impulse in fighting completion anxiety symptoms is to try to get his tape back immediately, to rewrite or remix the songs. When he can't retrieve the tape, panic sets in. Then it turns to terror. And when the writer can't get anybody on the phone to notify to ignore the "first version" because the "good version" is on it's way by messenger, he starts belittling himself and tearing his work apart.

One of my clients was experiencing completion anxiety recently, but didn't know it. After he'd finished a five-song demo he told me, "I blew it. It's junk. Nobody's gonna cut this. My girlfriend will hear it and leave me for someone with muscles."

Sound familiar? Writing a song takes a lot of courage. But so does finishing one. Even more so for an album. It takes a great deal of energy to work as hard as we do. We love it, we need it, but we also have to learn how to let go graciously and come down slowly.

Usually the way to get past one obsession is to replace it with another. But I find that when we finish a song, we can't just start another one right away. Like wheat fields, we need time to lie fallow, to regroup, to reenrich ourselves so we have fresh energy to draw upon when we next pick up our pencils.

I noted every step of my own letting go process recently after I had completed a project that I'd been working on every morning for six months. Once I delivered it to my producer, and had nothing else to do, here's what I did: cleaned out my refrigerator; polished all the mirrors in my house; went to a movie; unclogged my shower drain; Christmas shopped and got so anxious about the money I was spending that I returned everything I bought while double-parked and got a major ticket.

I didn't stop there. Then I had to prepare my plea for traffic court—not guilty, on the grounds of completion anxiety; bought two bestselling hardcover novels; felt betrayed by everybody leaving town even though I purposely sent them away so I could finish my project in peace; mashed trash; wondered how long it would take for my canker sore to become galloping gum disease since my dentist was at a root canal convention; and spent twenty-seven hours in bed, ate a box of fig newtons, and shivered.

I gave myself a few days to be crazy. But on day three, when I awoke and before my anxiety could switch into high gear, I jotted down the following:

It's a time of loose ends.
It's a time of self-doubt.

It's a time of self-deprecation.
It's a time of hypersensitivity.
A time of mood swings.
A time of childlike reactions and needs.

The elation that follows completion takes us out of our normal emotional "safety zones." Strung-out, far off course, we get scared and start to worry. Worrying and anxiety replace writing as our fulltime jobs.

Writing is a passion. Passion is obsessive. It is natural for a letdown to follow a good writing session. So understand the lull. Spend the time gently—float in the uncertainty. The world is not going to end with this project. It's *part* of your life's work—not *all* of it. You're a creative person, and you've got lots more inside you. Trust your inspiration to be there for you when you need it. But first, you have to give it a well-deserved rest. It's important that you recognize this time as part of your creative process, because it isn't until you can let go that you can truly move on to accepting constructive criticism, and then, when you're ready, starting another song.

Remember to pamper yourself during this process, giving yourself whatever you need to get through it. Whatever you do, don't trample yourself for not doing things "the way you should." This is a very delicate time for you, when you're called on to be nicest to yourself.

Realize that your song or album has not gone off and left you. It's just in the mail or on somebody's desk. Your job now is to separate yourself nicely from what you wrote. You are *not* your song or your album. You are just the person who created it, even if every syllable of the lyric is true.

Should negative thoughts arise, and they tend to think they have license to assault us on these sensitive days, push them away. Affirm all the good things about yourself.

Choose a physical task, like cleaning out the fridge or washing your car, and make a "project" out of completing it. That way, your energy is channelled into something with short-run, tangible results. In this way, you may actually allow yourself to feel like you've really achieved something.

PART
THREE

Doing Business
in the
Music Business

CHAPTER SIXTEEN

Doing the Hustle—Nicely

Now that you've worked so hard to rewrite and demo your songs, we have to address the issue of how to market them. No demo ever moved itself off the shelf, hitchhiked into Hollywood, and made the enthusiastic but endless rounds of publishing and record companies. Your work can't play itself for anyone who will listen, take new business connections to lunch, leave nice tips, get itself cut, campaign for a single, hire an independent promoter to get it into the top ten, and finally, cash its own six-figure royalty checks. But a lot of writers insist on believing their job is over once they've written their songs. It isn't. It's just beginning. Where writing ends, hustling begins. And I honestly believe the hustle is never over.

Most songwriters and singer/songwriters are terribly uncomfortable when it's time to switch gears and enter the business phase. However, the *successful* writers and singers have mastered the skills and concepts necessary to be as good at business as they are at creating.

As a writer, it's your job to know who's cutting, what they want, what they don't want, and when they want it. You might be thinking that's the publisher's job. But let me ask you something: has a publisher you've never met or with whom you haven't nurtured a relationship over a period of years, gotten any of your songs cut this week? I didn't think so.

A lot of gifted songwriters think those "yellow page books" listing every music publisher in the western world are all they need, and proceed to mail unsolicited tapes to everybody in the directory. Frankly, what those books do best is make money for their publishers by cashing in on songwriters' naïveté. The *real* music business, is not conducted by mailing massive tapes to strangers.

The key to your success in this business is how well you develop and nurture personal contacts, and keep them alive. If you don't have any "relationships," start making some. Be nice to the receptionists and gofers, because let me tell you something. The stuttering stock boys who couldn't complete a simple sentence and the do-dah receptionists with two-inch black fingernails whom I met during my staffwriting days are all presidents and vice presidents today. It boggles my mind that some of these people are even out of prison, but there they are on the letterhead. And they do business with people they know, or who are referred by people they know.

Do lunch. Send valentines. Call just to say hello, or to tell a joke. Many songs are good songs and deserve to be cut. But the ones that *are* cut usually are written by a songwriter who relentlessly hangs out socially with the producer or publisher— playing cards, golf, or tennis.

I used to know a songwriter who could have taught hustlers how to hustle. Even though he had capable professional managers to handle his tunes, this guy ran his own. And he got them all cut. He also did string charts for record dates and ingratiated himself with all the producers, so there was usually one of his own songs on their next date. He played keyboards for singers on their demos, and when these singers finally got deals, guess who had a tune on their albums? He used his boss's connections well, developing relationships of his own with everybody, and soon his publisher gave him a piece of the pie, which grew into stock in the company as that enterprise mushroomed and diversified.

Tom Sturgess of Chrysalis Music told me he has pitched tunes 100 times before getting them cut. As an unknown songwriter you should be willing to contact 100 publishers, not eighty-three or ninety-seven, but 100, before you quit on a song. Billy Steinberg ("True Colors," "How Do I Make You") told me he writes with his partner, Tom Kelly, half of each day, and then spends the other half going after records. And ninety percent of their songs are cut these days, which is phenomenal, considering neither Billy nor Tom currently sing their own songs. They hustle.

What do you do if you're not a natural hustler? You learn to be one. When my clients are starting from scratch and don't know anybody, I recommend they apply for an internship (an industry euphemism for slavery), and work for free for a little while in order to let people get to know how good they are. They're taken much more seriously on a creative level when people know them and feel comfortable with them.

I suggest you give yourself time to develop your contact and business skills just as you had to develop and hone your writing chops. Set aside time each week to make phone calls to potential business associates, and set aside more time each week to *call back*. Remember, without follow-up, nothing ever happens. Go to industry functions. But don't attend only one or two, or only the freebees—go to *all* of them. Shake hands with everybody.

Sometimes when writers finally learn to hustle, they can overdo it. If you're angry and frustrated because you've called eighty-six times and your call hasn't been returned, don't even consider trying to make the connection again until you've calmed yourself down enough to be gracious.

Another thing to remember—and this is crucial—is that many people who work in record and publishing companies have failed or quit as writers or artists and have opted for the safe paycheck. They have creative personalities, including the usual idiosyncratic bouquet of neuroses. So it's important to treat the people on the other side of the desk as sensitive artists, too. Be gentle with them and considerate of their feelings, problems, and agendas.

When you get a nibble what do you do? I don't mean to sound like my grandmother, but you make a cup of tea, dig for more worms, throw out more lines, and go after more nibbles. Hustling is an art, like writing. Knowing when to press and when to let go is as important as the song itself.

NETWORKING WORKS

There's another, nicer word for hustling—networking. I operate on the theory that everybody I know knows somebody I'd like to know and vice versa. My friends are smart and successful. They know other people just like themselves. When I want something that's out of my usual "need zone," I call a few associates and ask them who they know who would know somebody who can get me in touch with the people who can help me.

I didn't invent this process. In his biography *Hammer* (Putnam, 1988), Armand Hammer says that whenever he got involved in a new enterprise and he had many fields of interest—from medicine to pencilmaking to fine art—he always contacted someone at the the highest level he could. Networking.

What most songwriters forget is that the music business is a business. The industry has corporate ladders just like other businesses, even if the world headquarters of a particular company is a phone booth on Selma Ave. Songwriters' needs and passions are usually short-term. They want a hit *now*. They want the power brokers in the industry to recognize their talents *today*, while they're still ambulatory and before the next rent check bounces.

How do you get in the door if they don't know you and your connections aren't strong enough yet to penetrate the inner circle? Create a network of your own.

In the July 1989 issue of *Business to Business*, there's an article written by Sharon Hagelstrom, the president of Market-Pro America. She says that if you attend a major networking function, you may be successful, but only half as successful as you could be if you were also looking for leads for other people.

She suggests if you meet someone who has a need—an uptempo song for a single, for instance—and you don't have the song yourself but know of someone who does, go out of your way to put the people together. This person may never personally give you leads, but what goes around comes around. Your positive efforts will come back somehow, some way.

Operating on the theory that most people have a hard time receiving without giving back, if you do someone a favor, she will probably try to return it. So be direct about what you want. Don't just say you'd love to meet some publishers. Specify who.

Ms. Hagelstrom included several excellent marketing tips. They are:

1.   When you join an organization, don't just show up and sit at the back during meetings. Be active. Volunteer for jobs and committees.

2.   Show interest in the other people there. Don't just talk endlessly about how hot you are. Ask what other people write. They'll be flattered and you'll make a very good impression.

Don't ramble on. Be concise. Watch people's non-verbal language. If you see they're not interested and start backing away, switch the subject or end the conversation. The best salesmen find out as much as they can about the *other* person and plan to call them later at their offices. They don't move in for the kill on the spot.

3.   Don't just *take* business cards, *give* business cards. One sales trainer suggests giving out two. Why two? One to keep and one to give away to someone else. Be sure and tell the recipient the reason for the second card, otherwise it'll probably be trashed. Also, crimp the cards. Crimping the corners will make your cards stand out in a stack. It's also recommended that you hold the card near your adorable face for a second before handing over the card. That way, the person can associate your business card with the visual image of your aforementioned adorable visage.

4.   Follow up by mail or telephone within a week of meeting someone. If you can't follow up right away, write the date and location of your meeting on the back of each card. That way, if you call three months later, you'll be able to remind your new contact where and when you met.

5.   File the business cards you collect, alphabetically, by name or subject: A&R person; ambulatory standard writer in polyester leisure suit; airhead bottle blonde with tight, white T-shirt. This eliminates the risk of overlooking people who might be good resources just because you can't remember names.

6.   Don't limit your networking to business functions. You can meet people with whom you can do business at laundromats, Little League games, tennis tournaments, and parole hearings.

7.   Set a goal to make a certain number of new contacts at each function. Increase that goal at each subsequent function.

8. Make yourself noticed in a positive way. The person who says something funny or delivers his message in rhyme is more apt to be remembered.

9. Network regularly. If you only show up when you need business, you may not have any business when you need it. You should keep your name and face in front of people on a regular basis.

10. Send cards, especially thank you cards. Clip articles published about colleagues and send them a copy with a short personal note of congratulations. According to *Boardroom Reports*, the worst offenses business people make are: keeping someone waiting, failing to return phone calls, and forgetting to say thank you for favors or hospitality.

11. World-renowned speaker Mark Victor says you usually sell or don't sell yourself within four minutes after people meet you. So making a good impression is crucial. Here are some suggestions on how to do this:

- ◆ Get people's names correctly and reuse them in the conversation.
- ◆ Compliment their appearance if you can do it sincerely.
- ◆ Recognize any of their achievements or awards.
- ◆ Ask about their jobs and families. "So, how are things since the Time takeover?"
- ◆ Ask for their advice.
- ◆ Bring them business. Because bringing each other business is what networking is all about.

CHAPTER SEVENTEEN

Packaging = Power

Even though you now know how to rewrite and polish your songs until they sound like hits, just writing great songs isn't good enough anymore. If you look at the Hot 100 in *Billboard* this week, you'll see that ninety-five percent of the material on the pop chart is either sung by its writers, produced by its writers, or is in some way controlled through a package unavailable to you and me. While the percentages are a little less foreboding in country, gospel, and R&B, they're catching up fast.

So where does that leave us nonsingers and nonproducers? I hate to admit it, but the boom era of the independent songwriter is over. You might find a couple of brand name tunesmiths who don't produce or sing who are getting their material covered, but most of us have to rethink this whole process.

The reality of this situation hit me smack in the face when I recently started writing songs again, after a six-year hiatus. There I was with new material, mustering my courage, calling publishers I used to know, and for whom I even wrote *hits*, and they told me straight out that they're looking for singer/songwriters now, *not* just songs. So I sat myself down and said: "You're a terrific writer. You're committed to this, you've perfected your craft, you spent a thousand dollars each on these demos, you know the songs are hits, you'll have to find a way to make this work."

I decided then and there that all of us nonsinging, nonproducing writers (NSWs & NPWs) can't lie down dead and continue allowing the folks with more fortunate vocal chords to
dominate the business. I'm not suggesting we overthrow MCA
next Tuesday, but I do give all my clients the same advice: Become more entrepreneurial and develop packages with your material attached. That will guarantee you recordings. This will
turn your form rejection letters into personal phone calls asking,
"How soon can you get over here, baby?"

I suggest you find a terrific, up-and-coming group and
make them a business proposition: you'll cowrite their material,
and help *them* get a deal. They in turn, will be contractually
bound to record your songs. That way, you get your material cut,
and they get a deal they might not have gotten otherwise. Everybody wins.

I know that many of you are sensitive artists lacking both
the desire and the chutzpah to switch gears and become business
people. But actors are just as sensitive and all the successful ones
have their own production companies. They don't sit around
with $200 haircuts waiting for someone to offer them roles. They
develop the scripts themselves.

When I looked at the list of songs nominated in the best
song category for this year Grammys, I saw that every single one
of them was cowritten by the singer or group performing it. So,
if you don't create a home for your songs, you're making your
success dependent on somebody else's whim. But right now you
can increase your odds of having a hit *tenfold* if you take my
advice.

In the past I'd always hoped that one fine day, an eighteen-
wheeler full of crisp, new, $100 bills would pull up at my door,
donated by someone who simply liked the color of my eyes. But
so far, nobody's delivered anything I haven't fought for. So if I
want to compete in this marketplace today, I have to accommo-
date the new demands of that market. And so do you.

Let me use a tennis analogy. Chris Evert was the top
women's tennis player in the world. She had brilliant ground
strokes, used a wooden racket, and beat everybody. Then along
came Martina Navratilova who used a metal racket and played a
serve and volley game. She devastated Chris regularly. As good

as Chris was, and as successful as she'd been, she simply had to change her game or quit. Chrissie chose the former, and really challenged Martina for awhile. Now all the new players use metal rackets and nobody, including the number one player, Steffi Graf, ever tries to play a baseline game anymore. So all of us nonsinging and nonproducing writers have to change our games, too.

We know our songs are terrific. So we simply have to go one step further and find packages that guarantee their future. I think of my tunes as if they were my children: nothing is too good for them. I wouldn't mail my baby to some schnook I don't even know and hope he'll take care of it. *I'll* take care of it myself.

Nobody is more interested in the future of a song than its writer. Ever. So it's up to us to fight for what we want, and not wait for somebody to feel like playing Cinderella. I recommend you make a commitment to yourself and your songs to go out one night a week for the next six months or a year—however long it takes—scouring every club in your area code, looking for a person or band who sounds as good as the radio, and whose material could use your input. Go backstage. Tell the performers that you're a good writer. Tell them that you want to cowrite and help the group get a deal. The operative word here is *deal.* Then they can't say "Gee, thanks, but we write our own stuff." Many singer/songwriters are even worse at business than nonsinging writers because they're artists who expose their vulnerability on two levels. So here the nonsinging writers and nonproducing writers actually have an advantage over singer/songwriters.

When you find the act you want to work with and vice versa, have your lawyer draw up a contract and get everyone in the group to sign it. Don't go to all the trouble just to get axed at the last minute when the firm of Ego, Greed, and Slick gets involved.

You could argue that you'd just be perpetuating the closed shop mentally that's been excluding our songs. But frankly, I don't see anybody desperate to bump a self-written tune off an album in order to cut one of yours instead.

Writers usually don't have much control over their lives after the creating is done. But why not consider the packaging aspect of your writing as *something you're creating, too.* That way you *do* control the future of your work. You're not the victim of long odds and personal whims anymore.

If you still feel resistant to my idea, glance through the listings in all the music magazines and songwriter newsletters requesting material: every publisher, producer, and record label wants singer/songwriters. One of Leikin's Laws is give them what they want. Don't try selling oranges to a guy who wants tomatoes. And don't waste your time trying to sell tomatoes to a guy who's already got freight cars full rotting on the dock. But if you have what he wants, the gates fling open, and you can take whatever you want.

TAKING CONTROL

I'm not writing these recommendations for your reading pleasure. Unless you take the steps I'm suggesting, we both may be wasting our time. Here's how you go about it. First, make a list of all the local clubs where new bands and singer/songwriters appear. For the next six months, go see at least one group per week.

When you find a group whose material's style is close to what you write naturally, go backstage, introduce yourself, and suggest you write a couple of songs together, with a view to creating a whole album package afterwards. If they decline, and you really love what they write and how they sound, keep going back to see them. Take them out after the show for a drink. Once they are more comfortable with you, they could change their minds about your proposal.

Try and cowrite three songs with your new group or with a singer/songwriter. If the material you create together is top 10 caliber, and you want to work together on an album project, contact an entertainment attorney, and have an agreement drawn up.

Although this album may be your only priority, groups often have to travel for long periods, and they may get distracted. While your new partners are on the road, you should busy yourself making meaningful business connections at home. When your collaborators do get back, you'll be able to reinforce the value of your association through these new connections.

CHAPTER EIGHTEEN

How to Make Yourself Famous

Generating excitement about you and your work is critically important to every phase of a creative project. Even if you make a terrific deal with a major label or publishing company, the chances are that as a new artist, the signing of that deal will be ignored by the press unless you call their attention to it. It's a perfect opportunity for you to get a little publicity for yourself, so don't let it go by without doing something about it. Nobody is famous by accident. Getting yourself "known" is as important and as difficult, if not more so, than writing, singing, producing, and hustling your material.

During my scuffling days, a nice man from ASCAP's publicity department told me to get my name in the papers as much as I possibly could. Until then I naïvely thought that anyone who wrote as well as I thought I did would shortly be a household word. So from then on, every time I had a record released or wrote a TV theme, I issued a press release and the trades usually printed it. Fortunately for me, my surname was usually misspelled, so each publication had to print a correction in a subsequent issue, which made it look like I was working twice as much as I actually was.

When my first country hit was on the air, I was sure that

absolutely everyone in the media would be lining up three deep to interview me. But nobody did. Even though "Silver Wings and Golden Rings" garnered tons of airplay and become a big hit, it didn't have a *story* behind it that made it any different from all the other love triangle tunes on the radio. I realized too late that if I'd based the tale on a true story in which the real wife of the man in the song found out about our relationship, committed a mass-murder and used the song as her defense, *then* I would've had something to interest the press.

Some people hire expensive publicists to help them hype themselves. They pay these people exorbitant fees and sometimes it works. Bruce Springsteen's career didn't suffer at all from being on the covers of *Time* and *Newsweek* simultaneously. But those of you without the means to pay $2,500 a month and up should learn how to do your own inexpensive publicity.

Whatever you're trying to publicize has to have a "hook," just as your songs do. Think about it—there are a hundred songs on every chart, but how many of them are talked about outside the radio? And if you're not the artist, the songwriter is rarely, if ever, mentioned.

There are some publicity campaigns I've truly admired. Madonna's got a good voice. I've enjoyed a lot of her songs. But I wonder if we'd even know about her if she didn't dress so outrageously, pose nude in *Playboy,* and list herself in *Who's Who* as the one who doesn't shave under her arms. Her shaky marriage to a movie star who was always in trouble didn't hurt her any either. Neither did her controversial video "Like a Prayer." Without all the hype and PR, she could be just another sexy girl with a good voice who made good records. She could still be nobody, in spite of her talents.

In my first songwriting book, "How to Write a Hit Song," I chose to include "That's What Friends Are For" as a model of a well-structured AAB AAB song. When I called the publisher to get permission to use the tune, I was told it had been the theme for a successful movie called *Night Shift* four years earlier. The song had played over the end credits. I had seen the film, but didn't remember the song at all. I wondered if just maybe the publisher was smoking his socks a little early in the day. But I rented the video and sure enough, the melody to "That's What

Friends Are For" underscored the entire film. And the same lyric was sung over the end titles.

You might wonder how a song that was obscure for four years suddenly won a Grammy. Well, somebody made smart decisions. Following the trend of "We Are the World," four big artists who'd never recorded together were featured on the record in an effort to raise public consciousness about AIDS. So it wasn't just a record anymore. It was a phenomenon. And it certainly wasn't an *accident*. It was one of the most carefully and purposefully orchestrated media events of the decade.

When you write a song that gets released, you'd be smart to consider creating a story about how or why this song was written to make it more interesting than other songs, to give it some "media appeal." Cole Porter was a master songwriter and didn't have to hype his work. But I once read that when he was thrown from his horse and pinned under it, he pulled out his pencil and wrote "At Long Last Love" before help came. If I were a reporter, I'd want to write *that* story. It is more appealing a tale than "Ralphie dumped me for another chick and I was bummed so I scored some Ripple and wrote, like, this riff."

The publicist I hired to promote my first songwriting book told me that because it was soft cover and a "how-to," nobody in the western hemisphere was interested in doing stories or interviewing me about my book. So I fired him. Although I realized I would've done just as well taking the money I'd spent on this publicist and set fire to it, I believed in my book and was determined to make it a success. So I started calling the media myself. I set up fifty-six radio interviews, got three major stories in daily newspapers, which were syndicated nationwide, and booked myself on three national TV shows, all of which had initially turned me down at least three times.

You don't have to have anything as major as a book or an album or a staffwriting deal in order to get publicity. One of my clients in the Boston area owns an ice cream store and was desperate to sell it so he could write fulltime. I cautioned him against any rash moves, especially since he hadn't established any credibility yet as a songwriter. And so together we came up with a plan for him to get some momentum in the form of local publicity. He didn't have an advertising budget for his ice cream shop, so I suggested he contact a local top 40 radio station and arrange for them to do a remote from his store on Mother's Day, when he would give a complimentary cone to any mother who came in with her family. His pitch was "I want to give a free ice cream cone to every mother in Boston." And he got a radio station to cooperate immediately. My client wrote a special jingle for the occasion and it was played five times during the broadcast. That was good PR for the radio station, and great PR for my client, who got an assignment to write another jingle by the end of the day.

People in our industry skim the trades and daily papers for names so they know whose calls to take. They don't really read the articles. If your name appears in print, they suddenly think you're hot. While you're at any media event, be sure to look for the person with the camera. Getting your picture in the paper is the most valuable form of publicity. Nobody will care where the picture was taken, or why, they'll just remember you were seen.

There are some "songwriters" we know about who never write anything original but are brilliant at being everywhere and smiling on cue. They always manage to be standing next to or dating somebody famous, so they get their pictures and names in the papers a lot. And that translates into making their songs more desirable, because our industry operates on fear. Everybody's afraid of offending somebody who's important.

Most artists are not very good at promoting themselves and shudder at the thought of trying. But you should practice self-promotion every day, just as you vocalize and do your scales. The more you do it, the less frightening it becomes. Think of it this way—it's much more terrifying to be anonymous.

MAKE THE MEDIA NOTICE

Before you go off self-promoting your tunes, do your homework. Read your local newspaper entertainment section, and watch all the entertainment-oriented news segments on TV to see which artists and songs are being discussed. Study the media "hooks" that are used to make the song interesting and different from those tunes that aren't talked about. Make a list of names, addresses and phone numbers of all the local entertainment media people to contact.

Practice creating media "hooks" for your songs. There is something about each of you and every one of your songs that makes you and your work different from anybody else's on the planet. Figure out what that "hook" is, and practice "pitching" it in fifteen seconds or less, which is about all the time you'll have to interest anybody in the media when you call. For example: "I'm the illegitimate daughter of the Prince of Monaco and I wrote a song called "I Married Hitler's Son" and I'd like to talk to you about doing a story on the coup d'état I've planned in conjunction with the simultaneous release of the record and the coronation of my half-brother Prince Albert next Friday."

For practice, write a two-paragraph press release about one of your songs. For example, if you wrote a song as a wedding gift for Suzie, and when she heard the song, she decided to marry you instead, that would make a great local story. But don't just announce that you wrote a song for Suzie's wedding and leave it at that, unless the bride was a well-known celebrity.

Try to write a song that has "media" appeal and record it. Create a press kit, which includes a two-paragraph news release about the song, a copy of the song on cassette with the lyric sheet, a short bio with your resumé, a black and white 8″ × 10″ photograph, and a phone number where you can be reached.

Then, pitch your story to the local newspaper entertainment editor and the local TV and radio stations. One call isn't going to do it—you may have to call back ten times. If you're finally mentioned in the paper or on TV, give yourself ten points. If your story appears with a picture, give yourself another ten points. If nothing happens with the story, stay in touch with the local news reporters, because eventually you might come up with something they can use.

Save all newspaper clippings and videotape any TV news segments about yourself and your songs. Sending copies with the next project you're trying to pitch really validates you in the eyes of the media. Then a reporter can tell his editor "The guy who wrote Caroline Kennedy Schlossberg's baby's favorite lullaby has just made an album. Can we run a story on this?"

CHAPTER NINETEEN

Don't Be a Day Job Snob

When a person works as singlemindedly for as many hours a day as you do at songwriting, you'd expect to earn a living from your creative labor. Someday, you will. But until you have your first big money-producing cut, it's foolish to relinquish your ability to pay your bills.

Many new clients who come to me are desperate for instant success. They've just decided to make a serious commitment to their music and want to quit their regular jobs. Although I applaud their newfound devotion, I urge them, for the time being, to keep those jobs. I know this may sound discouraging. But it has nothing to do with talent. It simply has to do with the way cash flows in the music business.

While waiting to see a publisher I interviewed for this book, I met his receptionist who told me she was also a songwriter. She proudly announced that she'd cowritten a cut on a platinum album and she was even a staffwriter for a small publishing company. You're probably wondering what this woman was doing answering phones for minimum wage if she really had a tune on a platinum album *and* a gig as a staffwriter?

Well, six years ago, UPS delivered one of my gold records. I received the money today. Does that give you any clues?

I'd had other successful songs, but was a staffwriter during all the others, living comfortably on advances, so I never really monitored the income from my earlier work the way I did this time. Until the check arrived today, I would get several hundred dollars from the publisher each quarter. I'd call him up each time and ask when I could expect my windfall. "Soon as I get it, you'll get it," he told me. And this publisher was no scuzz-bucket, either. He was totally legitimate. Even so, it took six years for me to get my foreign mechanicals. So be aware that even when you *do* make some major money, it still takes forever plus a long weekend to actually *see* it.

We've all chosen to be songwriters because we love to write. But like all great passions, it's expensive. The more equipment we have, the more we need. Repairing and servicing it costs plenty. So does updating it. You have to have money *now* to afford all of this. And therefore, you need to have a real job to earn it.

But you're a songwriter, you tell me. You wonder why you should go out there and spend your life injecting collagen or rotating tires or both when you're an "artist"? The answer's simple. I've checked the want ads in the *Los Angeles Times* every day since arriving here eighteen years ago. Not once have I ever found an ad for a songwriter.

Living nicely in the meantime is not selling out. Struggling to pay the rent and buy groceries and clothes was romantic for twenty minutes or so. I've been rich and I've been poor, and rich is a big improvement. My assistant works thirty hours a week in addition to her full load as a senior at UCLA. She needs a car, insurance, books, clothes, haircuts, not to mention CDs, VCRs, and ongoing miscellaneous items like bagels and mayonnaise. And I bet you're no different. It might help if you think of your day job as money you're earning while "going to songwriting school," if you will, or putting in your apprenticeship. You'll be in good company.

I asked many of my favorite singer/songwriters, publishers, and record execs what awful jobs they'd had on their way to the top. Jimmy Webb ("By the Time I Get to Phoenix," "Up, Up and Away") made lead sheets for five dollars each and was the janitor in a dingy demo studio on Selma. Occasionally, he'd get lucky and play piano for twenty-five Rod McKuen or Lettermen tunes in one day, and earn a *total* of twenty-five dollars.

Epic A&R mogel Don Grierson told me he was a stock boy,

then a cashier at Music Plus. While he was working in the record store, he used his time wisely, studying buying trends, promotions, retail procedures—all of which helped him later in his career. He didn't roll into town and put his feet up, saying "I'm a record company executive so I'm going to stay home and wait until someone makes me a vice president."

J.D. Souther ("New Kid in Town," "You're Only Lonely"), told me he built houses, roofed houses, and painted houses. "I even sold shoes—boots, actually, at a mall in Amarillo, although they eventually fired me for givin' Dingos away to my friends."

Alan O'Day ("Angie Baby," "Muppet Babies"), told me he always—*absolutely always*—earned his living from music. "You never had a little part-time doing something else," I wondered. "Well, actually, I was a box boy," he admitted. "At the A&P in Indio, California. I started working there part-time. But then somebody who was fulltime quit, and I was promoted."

Billy Steinberg ("Like a Virgin," "True Colors") taught himself Spanish and oversaw the picking of grapes by eight hundred farm workers at his family's vineyard in Thermal, California. Half a world away, in Southampton, England, Martin Page ("These Dreams," "We Built This City") cleaned toilets, mowed lawns, and then became a professional soccer player. As for me, well, I was a social worker in the San Fernando Valley. Many of my clients were unwed mothers who claimed Elvis Presley or Paul McCartney was the father of their children, so at least it was an industry-related job.

Tom Selleck isn't a songwriter, but actors are artists who share our fiscal dilemmas. When he appeared on "Donahue" recently, Tom said he signed to do his "Magnum" series at $30,000 per episode, but before he got a dime, the actors went on strike. Absolutely broke, Selleck worked for his landlady for seven dollars an hour, painting and plastering. Here he was rich on paper —but in reality, until the strike was over, he was dead broke. And yet he wasn't afraid that nobody would think of him as an actor if he did odd jobs until the strike ended.

We've all had day jobs. If you don't have one, and need money, get one. Don't, whatever you do, just live on your credit cards, thinking you'll pay them off as soon as your ship comes in. The interest you pay on those cards would sink most ships. If there isn't a job you want, create one you do want. You've got an imagination, don't you? Here are some suggestions: somebody should open up a company called Roofers in the Rain, which will actually send a guy over before the next storm to *repair* the damage, not make it worse. If you want something closer to the ground, here's another suggestion. In a recent trip to Sedona, Arizona, I found that 94% of the locks on ladies room doors were either missing or needing repair. This problem is not indigenous only to Red Rock country. Somebody could fix the locks in Southern California, and franchise the rest of the continent to other songwriters in need of employment. The company could be called Rock Locks . . .

Leikin's Seventh Law is: when you have the money from your hit, *then* you quit. So keep your day job. It creates short-term income. Best of all, it'll give you something funny to talk about when you've finally made it and somebody is doing the next songwriting book, and wants to include a chapter about the strange odd jobs that famous writers have had.

CHAPTER TWENTY

Ethics in *This* Business?

Because you have to fight so hard and so long to get anything in the music business, when you start feeling like you'll never get anywhere, which we all feel from time to time, it's easy to let your moral principles slide. Maybe something comes up that you know isn't completely kosher, but you feel that just this once you're willing to look the other way. Don't. Someone told me if you walk in the gutter, you start to smell like garbage. And as an artist, your reputation is your most valuable commodity.

Throughout my whole life in the music business I've struggled with right and wrong and all the shades of gray in between. Some writers feel whatever they do is exempt from judgment as long as they get a hit. I passionately disagree. If a deal is dirty, the stain never washes out. You start to feel and act tainted, and then suddenly everything you fought for disappears.

In the '70s there was a hot producer who was notoriously greedy. If he couldn't get 100 percent of the publishing fee on a song that the record company wanted to release as a single, he'd "ask" the writers to make him their under-the-table writing partner. He "needed" to take a chunk of their royalties. His name wouldn't be listed as cowriter on the record labels, just the accounting statements, so nobody would know he'd done this. If the writers refused, he would remix the song so it sounded bad, and release a different single. Everybody caved in, giving him whatever he wanted, and he became fabulously wealthy.

That was my first encounter with sleaze, but certainly not my last. I once had a very talented publisher who came from nothing and finally got his chance to run a major company. Although he convinced his bosses he was ready for this challenge, he hadn't yet convinced himself. In spite of the fact that his job was to act as an editor of his staffwriter's songs, he insisted on taking percentages of our copyrights in exchange for his input. The first time this happened I was angry but terribly torn. I knew what he'd done was wrong, but he was my boss and I was afraid *I'd* be ostracized if I said anything. So I let it go. But the second time, I reported it, and the publisher was fired. I think he's the maitre d' at a chinese restaurant now.

Even though I was initially afraid to stand up for what was right, when I found the courage, I was vindicated. As wimpy as I was in those days, if I had it in me to blow the whistle on this sort of lapsed morality, everybody does.

Many years later, after having been commissioned to write an impressive array of TV and movie theme songs, I got a call from a producer asking me to write a theme for her TV movie. I said I'd be happy to, and suggested she call my attorney to work out my fee. But it seems that this production was experiencing some "financial tenderness" and didn't have any money left for such purposes. The producer expected me to write a lyric for no fee, and live on the hope for some big performance money. I knew that was a ridiculous proposition, since the song was to have been sung under the opening and closing credits. On a good day, without a feature performance, residuals would amount to about a dollar ninety-five—if she threw in some Fajita Pita coupons. I told her as nicely as I could that I'm a professional writer, that I do good work, that my songs win awards, and if she wanted one of those songs, she should expect to pay me handsomely to write it. If she wanted a freebee, she should ask a freebee writer to do a freebee job.

Cocky? Yes. But I felt I had the right. I had excellent, current credits. Besides, I was in the deep trenches with a group of my colleagues trying to form a union for screen and TV composers so we would *have* to be paid for our services. Slipping out in the middle of this momentous lawsuit to do a quick favor would've violated everything we were fighting for.

I have always felt enraged by producers asking songwriters to work on spec. I'd rather saw off my foot. Actors, screenwriters, and teamsters get paid for their work. So do directors, assistant directors, second assistant directors, unit publicists, grips, hair stylists, and dog trainers. So why shouldn't songwriters?

A few months later, the same producer called back. She told me she'd had four or five other lyrics written to the theme for her TV movie, but none of them was "right." She knew I'd give her exactly what she wanted, so she agreed to pay my fee. I wrote the lyric, which she claimed absolutely saved her project, and said of course she'd invite me to the recording session.

But the next day, the composer called to say they'd had the session without me. The reason I wasn't invited was because at this same session they also recorded four other lyrics written to the same melody and didn't want any of the lyricists present. The composer then told me that I shouldn't be upset because my lyric came out the best and they'd dubbed mine into the picture.

In spite of my "victory," I feel this producer's morals were bankrupt. She should have told me they were still considering the other lyrics, because I would've told her to make a decision about the others first before I wrote mine. But then my song from this movie was nominated for an Emmy, so this slimy story seemed to have a happy ending.

But five years later I arrived at another studio as the session ahead of mine was winding down. A tough little woman in fatigues who looked like Rambo's sister sauntered up to me with an attitude, shifted her weight from hip to hip and said, "Oh, *you're* Molly-Ann Leikin. You took work away from me." She told me she'd written four lyrics for that long ago Movie-of-the-Week, and was furious with me for horning in on her territory. I told her the producer had lied to me and I felt awful that this little Rambette would think I'd take a gig away from anyone. I had assumed they were unhappy with the other lyrics. That wasn't the case and she refused to hear my side of it. She'd been nursing her bitterness for five years and was looking for a fight.

Fortunately, someone in her group dragged her out of the studio before she rearranged any of my vertebrae.

I hope you learn from my experience that when collaborating, you should always ask the status of a lyric or melody, no matter who you're collaborating with and no matter what your own status happens to be. Don't assume you've been chosen because you're the only one on the planet with the sensitivity to do the job. Don't assume anything. Ask questions.

If somebody's already working on a particular project, you shouldn't contribute any work until the other lyric or melody has been completely turned down, no matter how hungry you are for exposure. And if the composer or lyricist wants to choose from several people's work, pass. I feel it isn't ethical to audition writers. The people we collaborate with are our colleagues, our partners, and we should behave and be treated as their equals, not as unknowns begging for a shot. It may seem ironic to have principles in a business which is often run like the mob, but hopefully behaving ethically will become as popular as health food and Past Life therapy.

By the same token, if you have a lyric or melody and need to collaborate, you should let one writer try a couple of drafts with it before you decide to take it back and give it to somebody else. This is perfectly legit, as long as the first writer knows you're doing it.

The best way to assure that your collaborative relationships don't go sour is to put everything in writing. This goes for those informal collaborations with "friends" as well. I know because I was recently betrayed by a close friend—let's call her Sheila Bonaduce.

I'd read a story of Sheila's that seemed like a perfect vehicle for a musical movie. She loved my songs and was flattered by my interest in her work. From then on we agreed that the project would be a musical and only a musical, and we'd be partners, fifty-fifty. I registered it as a joint work and sat with Sheila for weeks, rewriting the story with her, draft after draft, until it sizzled. We wrote up a new outline together, and since I'm more aggressive, I set up meetings at all the studios to "pitch" our project. One executive with whom we met loved it.

146 ◆ HOW TO MAKE A *GOOD* SONG A *HIT* SONG

He just needed to see one of Sheila's scripts as a sample of her writing before we got a "go."

The next day Sheila left a message on my answering machine saying she'd had an offer on the project without music. She'd accepted it and then refused to take or return my calls. Her agent told me she'd make sure I never worked again if I tried to block the deal. My lawyer said we could sue and win, but it would take nine years. He suggested I let it go and write something else.

We've all struggled with impatience and opportunity. Somebody fancier or more famous comes along and we know we could get lucky on his coat tails and there go the high moral principles.

I'm very sensitive to this issue. Like a lot of good writers, I've been burned by singer/songwriters who had other lyricists working on their tunes in secret. One musician and I spent six months writing an album together. We went to London for a month to record it, and when it was rejected by EMI, my partner, whose ego was enormous, blamed me, and dumped my lyrics without even telling me. And my own publisher scurried to find him another lyricist, who turned out to be a staffwriter at my same company. But EMI scrapped the rewritten project as well, and that artist hasn't had a successful album released since.

So treat your colleagues and partners with respect and consideration. Because what goes around comes around—in spades.

CHAPTER TWENTY-ONE

Tips from the Top

Now that you know how I feel about doing business in the music business, I think it would be helpful to hear from some other very successful songwriters and industry executives. All of them agree that this is a business of relationships. You can never know too many people who are well-placed and think highly of your work. The dictum, "It's not *what* you know but *who* you know" really applies in the music industry. Learn this early so you don't begin to believe that the quality of your work is necessarily the reason a relative stranger rejects you.

Even with connections you have to be a savvy business person. Jimmy Webb is suspicious, "I've paid a lot of good people top money to push my songs and it didn't pay off. Now I run my own. Last year, I got twenty-four cuts."

A lot of Webb's success results from knowing *who* to go to with his material. "You have to be absolutely sure in your heart that a song is right for an artist because you can't go back to the well too often," he advises. "If I tell Streisand I've got a song that'll go top 10 and she doesn't like it, she won't see me next time. So I'm very careful when I pitch a song."

Especially in today's volatile economic climate, in which corporations swallow each other whole and break apart with terrifying frequency, it's important to choose your business collaborators carefully. "I'd warn people against these big publishing companies," recommends Webb. "A person can make a lot of money running one of these companies into the ground and then jumping ship."

Barry Mann admits, "It's hard to get records these days. If I were starting out now, I don't honestly know how well I'd do." His advice to new songwriters who aren't artists themselves? "Learn to be a producer, too. Writer/producers are what's happening," Mann maintains.

Mann also believes beginners shouldn't get too pushy. "A lot of young writers say they're looking to split their publishing with a publisher. But it's not *their* publishing to split," he states. If a publisher is a good publisher, and does his job, he does the hustling, gets the records and does all the paperwork. Why should a writer get half of the publisher's money? The writer should get the writer's share and the publisher should get the publisher's share. Each gets fifty percent. Don't expect a good publisher to do all the work for half the money."

Don Grierson, the director of A&R at Epic Records, told me it would make it easier for A&R people everywhere to say "yes" to new writers and singers if they would realize three things when they're preparing a tape to submit:

1. Most tapes have too many songs on them. No A&R person has time to listen to fifteen tunes. Five is the maximum. Four is better. Three is ideal.

2. The tapes should be demos, not masters. A songwriter should be trying to showcase his songs, not his production chops. A good tune can get lost in an amateur production, no matter how slick a writer thinks he is, no matter how long he's in the studio futzing with a track, and no matter how much money he spends on the venture. A&R people are looking for good *songs*. Executives like Don know the producers that can turn your song into a hit record, so let *them* make the masters.

3. Epic, like all other labels, is looking for talent and originality, not just writers and singers who can copy what's already on the radio.

Publisher Tom Sturgess feels a writer has to separate himself from his song the minute it's written. "Cut the cord," he admonishes. "You plug the song, you send it out, sure, but it should be like it isn't yours anymore. You have to let the distance develop between you and your song. Ninety-nine people are going to say no before the one guy says yes. So you have to protect yourself, or the dream will be over."

"The most important thing is the relationship, not the record," Sturgess believes. "You'll write lots of songs. Establish your relationship for the long run, so the future will hold some promise."

Sturgess has his own method for dealing with the business. "I make myself a very easy person to say no to. If I make it easy for a producer, I make it easy on myself, too." And to prove it, Tom showed me a pitch card dating back to the first time he contacted Clive Davis in 1981. It took three years and twenty-seven no's from Clive before Tom got his first cut with the man. Now he hears a "yes" after every three or four songs, instead of the twenty-seventh.

"If he tells me why he didn't like the song, it helps me do better next time. I look at a 'no' as an opportunity to improve, to learn. If someone says he loved the chorus, I go back and listen to it and learn what kind of chorus he likes." Sturgess has realized that "Once he says 'no,' it's over. I don't try to sell a great bridge once he's made the decision."

Suzanne Vega is a folk singer who was fighting windmills, trying to be a star at a time when disco was king. She learned to keep a mailing list and send out flyers every time she had a gig, and developed personal connections with people in her audience, writing notes to her loyal fans on the flyers she mailed.

Even after Suzanne had a manager who was absolutely committed to her they got turned down everywhere. By everyone. A&M said no—twice. But Suzanne was very practical about it, "I didn't want to shove myself into a place where I wasn't appreciated."

However, she kept getting good press, and Ron Fierstein, her manager, kept sending the reviews to A&M. He believed if they just read how well the public thought Suzanne was doing, the people at A&M would change their minds. Finally, the *New York Times* wrote a wonderful review of Suzanne's act, and Ron sent it to A&M. They sent their New York A&R person to see her. And then they said yes. In 1988, Suzanne won a Grammy for "Lukka." So persistence paid off.

Randy Goodrum is a low-key, self-taught hustler and is charming as many Southerners can be. Rather than send demos, Randy invites producers to his house and plays his songs live. At least, he says, "You get a quick answer." If the producer won't come by, Randy makes a demo "for the general pitching program," but only reluctantly.

"If your focus is just to get songs cut, it's the wrong motivation. You should write because you love to write," Goodrum believes.

"Whenever you get a lemon, make lemonade. Don't sit around waiting for the mail. *Do* something," he advises. Randy is always learning something new. During a year-long dry spell, he taught himself how to be an engineer, which helps him make better demos.

Christopher Cross is very adamant, "To do well in this business, you have to meet certain requirements. It's like wanting to be in the NBA; you can't be 5'6" and be successful. To pursue music as a career, you have to have genius, passion, and something unique."

Narada Michael Walden feels one ability helps another: "Being athletic strengthens your heart and mind. When you're physical and try to transcend yourself it makes the soul happy. The soul is where the music comes from. It's the God in you. Let God's music come down to the earth. You have to push yourself to keep all the windows and doors open. Sports and dancing help do that. The push gives you an opportunity to sweat." And that's very healthy for the creative process. It also gives you momentum to call people who don't know you but with whom you would like to do business.

To Martin Page, a writer must convey integrity to his business associates: "It's not just hustle. They sense in you a desire to do well. Overpowering that even more is the enthusiasm you have for your work. It's like buying a car—you know the guy's trying to sell the car, but you want him to win you over. You wouldn't sell a four-door station wagon to a teenager buying his first wheels. It's the same with matching song and singer."

The worst thing a songwriter can do, according to Page, is try to copy what's on the radio. "An artist should have the courage to step out of his safety zone. You have to fall on your face now and then. That makes you a better artist."

Page points to the songs "Bridge over Troubled Water," and "Abraham, Martin and John" as examples. "They were written from an honest, emotional point of view. When we listen to these songs, we all feel that emotion. It makes us shiver. As a song-writer you want that response to be everlasting."

Publisher Linda Perry won't see anyone without a referral but she'll see anyone referred to her by someone she respects. She lives by a code of taking chances. "You never know where that hit is going to turn up. I fight for my songs. I fight for my writers." She says if you have talent, it will always surface. However, she believes "there are lots of cry babies who are full of shit out there. Not everyone is as talented as they like to think they are."

Lyricist Hal David cautions, "You're going to write more songs that don't work than do. The best you can hope for is a good percentage. Even at your peak, a hit or two a year is the best you can hope for." He advises that you go out and find an artist and package your material as I suggested in Chapter 17. "That's the only way to have control of your work," David insists.

Jeff Barry feels that, as writers, "we play to greed and jeal-ousy. A&R people want to think your songs will make money and artists want to cut them before someone else does." As charming as Jeff is, he's also a realist: "In the music business, people don't say hello unless it's good for them. A&R people don't know anything, and they know they don't know anything, so you're job is to give them confidence."

Jeff wears very stylish clothes. "Dress is important," he says. "The way you look from the neck down tells who you are. What you put out image-wise is what you attract."

Bunny Hall writes with artists and producers, so she doesn't have to submit songs to publishers. In the case of "Breakdance," she wrote it with Irene Cara and Georgio Mo-rodor. She also writes with producer Narada Michael Walden.

But she didn't always have access to them. When she arrived in Los Angeles, she didn't know anybody, and went to publishers and was turned down relentlessly. But since Bunny is a vocalist, she managed to work doing a lot of background singing. So she was in the studio with the very people she wanted to reach. And it worked.

You'll notice that none of the people I interviewed relies on anybody else to "save" or "discover" them. They are all actively involved in the business end of the music business. I recommend that you give serious thought to your responsibilities to the marketing side of your songs and rethink the whole business process. As soon as you realize it's really only up to you, you can have everything you want.

And you can take *that* to the bank.

Clichés

Try not to let any of the following phrases slip their way into your song lyrics. Perhaps if you work hard enough to come up with your own way of describing a thought or feeling, your expression may end up on a list like this in a few hundred years.

"Add insult to injury"—Phaedrus, *Fables* (c. A.D. 8).

"All dressed up with nowhere to go"—William Allen White (1916).

"All hell broke loose"—John Milton, *Paradise Lost* (1667).

"All is for the best"—Voltaire, *Candide* (1759).

"All's fair in love and war"—Francis Smedley, *Frank Fairlegh* (1850).

"All that glitters is not gold"—Alain de Lille, *Parabolae* (c. 1202).

"Be all and end all"—William Shakespeare, *Macbeth* (1605).

"Beauty's but skin deep"—John Davies, *A Select Second Husband for Sir Thomas Overburie's Wife* (1606).

"Bed of roses"—Christopher Marlowe, *The Passionate Shepherd to His Love* (1593).

"Better late than never"—Livy (59 B.C.–A.D. 17), *History*.

"Birds of a feather"—Robert Burton, *The Anatomy of Melancholy* (1621).

"Bite on the bullet"—Rudyard Kipling, *The Light That Failed* (1890).

"Bite the hand that fed them"—Edmund Burke, *Thoughts and Details on Scarcity* (1800).

"Blood is thicker than water"—John Ray, *English Proverbs* (1670).

"Captains of industry"—Thomas Carlyle, chapter title in *Past and Present* (1843).

"Charity begins at home"—Terence (c. 190–159 B.C.), *Andria (The Lady of Andros)*.

"Charmed life"—William Shakespeare, *Macbeth* (1605).

"Die for love"—William Shakespeare, *All's Well That Ends Well* (1601).

"Do or die"—Thomas Campbell, *Gertrude of Wyoming* (1809).

"Do as I say, not as I do"—John Selden, *Table Talk* (1689).

"Drop in the bucket"—*The Bible, Isaiah 40:15.*

"Dull as dishwater"—Charles Dickens, *Our Mutual Friend* (1865).

"Everyone to his own"—Angelus Silesius, *The Cherubic Wanderer* (1657).

"Eye for an eye"—*The Bible, Exodus 21:24.*

"The fair sex"—Miguel de Cervantes, *Don Quixote* (1605).

"Fallen from grace"—*The Bible, St. Paul's Epistle to the Galatians 5:4.*

"Fast and furious"—Robert Burns, *Tam O'Shanter* (1793).

"Feather our nest"—*Respublica* (1553).

"Few and far between"—Thomas Campbell, *The Pleasures of Hope* (1799).

"A few honest men"—Oliver Cromwell (1643).

"Fish out of water"—Thomas Shadwell, *A True Widow* (1679).

"Flat as pancakes"—Thomas Middleton, *The Roaring Girl* (1611).

"Foregone conclusion"—William Shakespeare, *Othello* (1605).

"Fresh as the month of May"—Geoffrey Chaucer, *The Canterbury Tales* (c. 1387).

"Gave up the ghost"—*The Bible, Luke 23:46.*

"Green-eyed monster"—William Shakespeare, *Othello* (1605).

"Hair of the dog"—John Heywood, *Proverbs* (1546).

"Hard as nails"—Charles Dickens, *Oliver Twist* (1837).

"Head over heels"—Gaius Valerius Catullus, *Carmina* (c. 60 B.C.)

"Heart to heart"—Walter Scott, *The Lay of the Last Minstrel* (1805).

"His bark is worse than his bite"—George Herbert, *Jacula Prudentum* (1651).

"Hitch your wagon to a star"—Ralph Waldo Emerson, *Society and Solitude* (1870).

"How the other half lives"—George Herbert, *Jacula Prudentum* (1651).

"In the cool of the day"—*The Bible, Genesis 3:8.*

"Iron hand in a velvet glove"—Charles V (1500–1558).

"It is in giving that we receive"—St. Francis of Assissi (c. 1226).

"It was Greek to me"—William Shakespeare, *Julius Caesar* (1598).

"The kiss of death"—Al Smith, referring to Hearst's support of a political opponent (1926).

"Labor of love"—*The Bible, St. Paul's Letter to the Thessalonians 1:3.*

"Lay it on thick"—Samuel Butler, *The Way of All Flesh* (1903).

"Live and learn"—Miguel de Cervantes, *Don Quixote* (1605).

"Look before you leap"—John Heywood, *Proverbs* (1546).

"Make the angels weep"—William Shakespeare, *Measure for Measure* (1604).

"Make the most of it"—Patrick Henry (1765).

"Man after his own heart"—*The Bible, Samuel 13:14.*

"Merry month of May"—Richard Barnfield, *Poems: In Divers Humours* (1598).

"The more the merrier"—John Heywood, *Proverbs* (1546).

"The morning after"—George Ade, *The Sultan of Sulu* (1902).

"Muddle through"—John Bright (1811–1889), in speech given during American Civil War.

"My dear, my better half"—Philip Sidney, *Arcadia* (1580).

"Never look a gift horse in the mouth"—St. Jerome (A.D. 420).

"Never-never land"—James M. Barrie, *Peter Pan* (1904).

"No man is an island"—John Donne, *Devotions upon Emergent Occasions* (1624).

"Nose to the grindstone"—John Heywood, *Proverbs* (1546).

"One foot already in the grave"—Plutarch, *Morals* (c. A.D. 120)

"One man's poison is another's meat"—Beaumont and Fletcher *Love's Cure* (1647).

"Pack up your troubles"—George Asaf, *Pack up Your Troubles in Your Old Kit Bag* (1915).

"A penny for your thoughts"—John Heywood, *Proverbs* (1546).

"Penny wise and pound foolish"—Edward Topsell, *Fourefooted Beasties* (1607).

"Pie in the sky"—Joe Hill (1879–1915), *The Preacher and the Slave.*

"Pig in a poke"—T. Tusser, *A Hundred Good Points of Husbandry* (1557).

"Pillars of society"—Henrik Ibsen, *Pillars of Society* (1877).

"Plain as a nose in a man's face"—François Rabelais, *Gargantua and Pantagruel* (1552).

"Pound of flesh"—William Shakespeare, *The Merchant of Venice* (1596).

"Powers that be"—*The Bible, Romans 13:1*

"Practice what you preach"—Plautus (254–184 B.C.), *Asinaria.*

"Red as a rose"—Samuel Coleridge, *The Ancient Mariner* (1798).

"Rough but ready"—Charles Dickens, *David Copperfield* (1849).

"Ships that pass in the night"—Henry Wadsworth Longfellow, *Tales of a Wayside Inn* (1863).

"The short and the long of it"—William Shakespeare, *The Merry Wives of Windsor* (1601).

"Sink or swim"—Thomas Starkey, *England in the Reign of Henry VIII* (1538).

"Six of one and half a dozen of the other"—Frederick Marryat, *The Pirate* (1836).

"Smell a rat"—Miguel de Cervantes, *Don Quixote* (1550).

"Snug as a bug in a rug"—Benjamin Franklin (1772).

"Sweetness and light"—Jonathan Swift, *Battle of the Books* (1704).

"Take it as it comes"—William Gilbert, *The Gondoliers* (1889).

"Three sheets in the wind"—Pierce Egan, *Life in London* (1821).

"Throw out the baby with the bath"—George Bernard Shaw, *Pen Portraits and Reviews* (1909).

"To have and to hold"—*The Book of Common Prayer* (1928).

"Tomorrow will be a new day"—Miguel de Cervantes, *Don Quixote* (1605).

"True blue"—Samuel Butler, *Hudibras* (1663).

"Two heads are better than one"—John Heywood, *Proverbs* (1546).

"United we stand, divided we fall"—American Revolutionary watchword (c. 1768).

"Upper crust"—Thomas Haliburton, *The Clockmaker* (1835).

"Vicious circle"—*Encyclopedia Britannica* (1782).

"Walk on eggs"—Thomas Heywood, *A Woman Killed with Kindness* (1607).

"Wild-goose chase"—William Shakespeare, *Romeo and Juliet* (1594).

"With a grain of salt"—Pliny the Elder (A.D. 23–79), *Natural History.*

Having read through this abbreviated list of well-worn phrases, you may be certain of two things: there are many, many more clichés than appear here; and it is likely that the authors or speakers cited as sources, in most cases, borrowed their words or thoughts, in some form, from somebody else.

I am grateful to the National Sanitary Supply Company for printing the "cliché calendar" from which many of these are quoted. I also would like to acknowledge *Bartlett's Familiar Quotations,* revised 15th edition, for serving as a reference and fact-checking source.

Leikin's Seven
Laws of Songwriting*

I **Banality bombs.**
Keep your clichés to yourself.

II **Sing it the way you say it.**
Unless you use phrases like "turtle dove" in everyday speech, don't use them in your songs.

III **Don't force a rhyme at the wrong time.**
It is more important to say what you mean than to say something meaningless because it rhymes.

IV **Write something that hasn't been heard before.**
Express age-old feelings through judicious use of the newest vocabulary in the English language.

V **Don't wait for parental approval.**
Write your songs for yourself. The hits will follow.

*According to Moses, you need to follow ten commandments; to write a hit song you only need seven. What a deal!

VI   **Give them what they want.**
Don't push country ballads to a heavy metal group, and don't write melodies with notes outside the singing range of the average recording artist.

VII   **Don't quit your day job.**
It's better to keep eating and sleeping indoors, on a Beautyrest Extra-Firm, at least until the money from your hit songs is safely deposited in your bank account.

If you would like information on how to schedule a private consultation with Molly-Ann Leikin to evaluate your material and help you develop a marketing plan for it, write to her office and request a brochure, which includes her fee schedule and an order form for her audio tapes. The address is:

Songwriting Consultants Ltd.
2210 Wilshire Blvd. #882
Santa Monica, CA 90403.